WALKING
IN THE
POWER
OF THE
ALMIGHTY
CREATOR

Luis A. Gonzalez

WESTBOW
PRESS®
A DIVISION OF THOMAS NELSON
& ZONDERVAN

WestBow Press books may be ordered through booksellers or by contacting:

WestBow Press
A Division of Thomas Nelson & Zondervan
1663 Liberty Drive
Bloomington, IN 47403
www.westbowpress.com
1 (866) 928-1240

ISBN: 978-1-9736-5394-3 (sc)
ISBN: 978-1-9736-5395-0 (hc)
ISBN: 978-1-9736-5393-6 (e)

Library of Congress Control Number: 2019901881

Print information available on the last page.

WestBow Press rev. date: 4/18/2019

I dedicate this book to my heavenly Father, the God of my youth and strength, the Lord Almighty.

Special Thanks and Acknowledgments

Clergy
Bishop Francis Anthony Quinn
Father Tom Vital Martin
Pastor Dick Bernal
Pastor Adam Bernal
Pastor Brian Cassidy (retired)

Family and Friends
To Rose and my children, Julius, Victoria, and Edson
My foster parents, Anita and Don Martin
The Martin family
My parents, Ana Rodriquez and Miguel A. Gonzalez
My siblings, Michael, Jacqueline, and Xiomara
Boniface, Preston, and Giselle Ojo
Annie, Tony, and Lisa Bryant, Jennifer Pumpetch, Isidro Sterling
Jackie Burga, Cathy Spiteri, Joshua Klein
Melissa and David Zraik, Terri Mertz, Navi Radjou

Contents

Names of God

The King of Kings

The Lord of Lords

The Ancient of Days

The Most High God

The Lord of Hosts

The King of Glory

The Lord God Almighty

The Everlasting God

The Lord, The Lord God

The Fountain of Living Waters

I Am, I Am That I Am

The Alpha and Omega

Abba Father, Heavenly Father

The God of the Whole Earth

The King of Angels

God, God the Father

The Creator, The Almighty

The God of Hope

The God of Abraham, Isaac, and Jacob

Elohim

Adonai

El Shaddai

Jehovah-Yahweh

Jehovah Nissi

Jehovah Rapha

Jehovah Sabbaoth

Jehovah Shammah

El Elyon

Jehovah Jireh

Jehovah Tsidkenu

El Olam

Jehovah Shalom

Jehovah Maccaddeshem

Jehovah Rohi

El Roi

Preface

In the spring of 1994, while I was a student at the City College of San Francisco, a most remarkable and extraordinary event happened: I had a real-life, physical encounter with the being known as the Creator. I was touched by His divine power and by the true revelation of His existence, and I was never quite the same any more. This dramatic event changed my life literally overnight and placed my outlook on the world in a new perspective.

Because of this incredible experience with the deity, I began to search for answers about Him and had a new interest and curiosity in finding out and discovering more about this God who manifested Himself to me. I believe the world deserves to know the truth about His existence, His awesome might and power, His passion for justice and truth, and His unfailing love for humanity. I would like to share this story with you before I leave the earth and this information dies with me.

Over the past twenty years, I have learned how to communicate with the Creator, who is known as the Lord of all the earth, and you also can learn how to communicate with Him and how to hear and recognize His voice. I have learned how to walk in His power while having His divine presence guide and protect me wherever I go. If you have ever wondered if the Creator of the universe exists and if He is even real, I am here to tell you that He is very real and really does exist because I have personally met Him, and it has changed my life.

This is one of the reasons why I wrote this book for you. One of the most important things I have come to realize is that the Creator is concerned about you and me and wants to be a part of our lives. He does this by helping us get through our challenges and struggles and by guiding us each day, so we can make the best choices and decisions along the way. This intimate relationship with Him will enable us to achieve and fulfill our desires and dreams in accordance with His will and divine plan.

> *If we will not be governed by God, then we will be ruled by tyrants.*

> —William Penn

Introduction

*Let us therefore come boldly to the throne of grace,
that we may obtain mercy and find grace to help in
time of need.*

—Hebrews 4:16 (NKJV)

I would like to share with you how the encounter with the Creator happened. I had recently graduated from the City College of San Francisco's department of aeronautics and was now working on my associate degree at the local community college. I found myself having an unusually tough time in a financial accounting class and was struggling and very frustrated. I was also not happy with the direction my life was taking at the time, so one afternoon, I got very angry and began shouting out loud in my apartment, "Almighty Creator, the message is for you! Almighty Creator, the message is for you! Almighty Creator, the message is for you!" Three times I said this as I pointed to the ceiling, and then I began to list my grievances to the Creator about my financial accounting class, my personal problems, and my general unhappiness. I went on this way for about twenty-five minutes, shouting a laundry list of complaints and grievances.

I said to the Creator, "If You are who You say, then prove Yourself to me, show me that You are real, and speak to me in an audible voice."

Suddenly, as I was about to take my next breath, the most peculiar thing happened: A strong gust of wind, or what I like to call a summer breeze, swept right through my apartment with great force. This surprised me because I did not have a fan or air-conditioner, and the door and all the windows were closed. As I turned around to see where this wind came from, I felt another wind. The first one was transparent in nature, but I could actually see it this time. It was like a large wave of water coming toward me, which rushed right past me.

As I was pondering and thinking about this mysterious and unusual wind that just swept over me, I then experienced someone opening a door in the back of my head; this force was attempting to get access to my mind. I thought to myself, *That's very odd and strange*, and I knew instinctively that something profound was about to take place.

Honestly, I became a little anxious and frightened, anticipating the unexpected, thinking perhaps I had crossed some kind of line with my complaining, and I felt I was no longer in control. I was not sure what would happen next. That's when an audible voice began to speak to me from three different directions. He then revealed to me and said, "I am your Father, your heavenly Father, the Creator."

As He spoke to me, I felt the nature of His masculinity and awesome power; I discerned His incredible love for us and His vast understanding, which appeared to reach into infinity. I was astonished. I could not believe this was really happening and said to myself, *My goodness. He is really real.*

I had an experience with Him as a child, when He first spoke to me as I was growing up; however, that was many years ago, and although I heard His voice, I never really saw Him. Up to this point, I was not really sure if He actually existed, because as a college student, I had learned to trust the opinions of PhDs, college professors, and the scientific community for answers, but now that had all changed in a dramatic moment.

This meant I would now need to reevaluate my beliefs and factor into the equation the existence of this immortal and divine being and take Him into careful consideration as I moved forward in life. I was also able to see the Creator as He spoke to me; He had the appearance and persona of a commander and of an ancient king.

He said only three things to me, which I will never forget: "I am sorry for the way you feel. I understand, but if I had given you everything, it would not have been fair to the others."

He then immediately showed me a vision. That was all the Creator said, but while He was speaking, I perceived a real and undeniable sense of His divine nature, His immense and unlimited power, and His great love for us, which appeared to go on for miles and miles without end. He also showed me His love and passion for justice, which startled me and got my attention and revealed to me His vast understanding of everything in the universe.

As I marveled at the Creator speaking to me, I was able to see Him clearly and determined that we were made in His image and likeness. He then showed me in this same vision other people around the world on different continents, including Europe, Asia, and the entire Western Hemisphere. These were people I didn't even know, people who were struggling with their own problems and issues. He made me understand that I was not alone and that everyone at some point in their life struggled and faced trials of some sort, but He was there to help if you were willing to call upon His name.

In the vision, I was also shown outer space and saw other planets in the distance, and then I was shown what looked like some kind of gigantic blue caterpillar or wormlike structure in outer space. This structure appeared to house some sort of advanced intelligence; I'm still not sure why I was shown this or what it means, even to this day, but I felt and understood that it was some kind of command center where decisions are made. The Creator showed me that we are not alone on planet Earth and that there is other intelligent life out there in the universe. I got the sense that He frequents that area in space, and I also understood that a part of Him dwells in us here on earth.

When this experience of the vision and the words He spoke were over, I was physically touched by His divine power and experienced a peaceful and warm feeling all over. I had this sensation that everything was going to be all right and that my prayer had been heard and would be answered. I then became peaceful and calm. After He touched me with His power, He never left me. He has been with me ever since. I truly believe the Creator, who is the God mentioned in the Bible, would want me to share this story about the truth of His existence so people don't lose hope when times get tough and difficulties mount. His desire is that you will put your trust in Him and call upon Him when all else fails and when you are feeling hopeless.

Simply put, He is a Father. He has a sense of fairness and desires to hold the hands of His children as they walk through their journey of life. He is there to help you make the best choices during critical times, so you get the most out of life, while keeping you safe and drawing you closer to Him. I have come to realize over the years that you don't need to have all the answers right away as you travel through life, but you do need to know the one who holds the answers, and in His perfect time, He will reveal to you what to do in each situation and every circumstance so that your life will be more fulfilling and will unfold in accordance with His will and divine plan.

> *Trust in the Lord with all your heart, and lean not on your own understanding; in all your ways acknowledge Him, and He shall direct your paths.*
>
> —Proverbs 3:5-6 (NKJV)

Chapter 1

The Art of Walking with God: A New Beginning

Noah was a just man, perfect in his generation. Noah walked with God.

—Genesis 6:9 (NKJV)

I would like to begin each chapter with a short teaching and an explanation on why that particular lesson is important. Once you understand and learn the significance of each chapter, you can then apply the techniques outlined within the reading and begin in time to experience supernatural, spiritual, and divine interactions in your life. At the end of each chapter, I will share a few short stories to illustrate where divine intervention and the miraculous became possible as a result of the lessons I have learned.

We are living in an age where advancements in technology are changing the world faster than ever before; this has transformed the way we do business, live, and interact with others. As you may know, every six months or so, we are seeing new devices, inventions, and gadgets introduced at record speeds. The acquisition of all these technologies, if we aren't careful, can end up consuming our precious time and resources. As a result, countless people are scrambling to keep up with the latest and greatest version of these new wonders, whether they are cell phones, cameras, electronic devices, or apps. An enormous amount of money, time, and energy is spent on acquiring these new gizmos. We are also seeing an explosion in entertainment opportunities, whereby you can enjoy movies, TV, news, and games on your phone, iPad, or computer, just about anywhere you go, and enjoy this entertainment right in the palm of your hand. This capability was unheard of twenty-five years ago, when I was just a kid.

The other day, I walked into a Best Buy store to purchase a couple of things. I had not been in that store for well over a year and a half, and I was so shocked by all the new products; for a split-second, I actually thought I had time-traveled into the future. It took a couple of seconds to realize this was not the case. These are all wonderful things to have, and they do make our lives easier, convenient, and more enjoyable. I use some of these gadgets myself.

But we must be careful not to fall into the trap of just seeking pleasure and worshipping technology in place of our Creator. The God of heaven would also like some of your time, talent, and resources. It's important that we don't get caught up in this frenzy by spending all of our free time entertaining ourselves and all our financial resources acquiring all the latest gadgets. Our Creator, who is a jealous God, desires devotion and requires we spend quality time with Him. There is nothing wrong with getting some well-deserved rest and recreation. However, I have witnessed many friends, acquaintances, and just regular people spending a lot of their free time doing things that are unfruitful or that don't add value to their lives, and then ten years later, they're wondering how they got to where they are at.

Time is very precious, and it's something you can never get back. As your personal time is important to you, so how you use it is equally important in the eyes of God. Some folks appear only to be concerned with making money when it is just as important to invest in their spiritual growth and development. My friend, you will need godly wisdom to help you manage your wealth, fulfill your dreams, and live within your means as you reach for new levels. Without this guidance, you can quickly end up on a street corner with a sign asking for help or living paycheck to paycheck in uncertainty.

Also, when we only desire financial gain and use it selfishly on ourselves instead of using it to be a blessing to others, we can easily fall into the trap of what the Lord calls worshipping the idols of silver and gold. This is what can happen when the pursuit of money becomes your idol, and that is what life can look like when you spend your life only pursuing financial gain. Simply put, the God of heaven wants to be worshipped above all things. Let's be mindful of that by not letting technology, entertainment, and making money get in the way of realizing his existence and spending quality time worshipping our true source, the Lord of Lords.

One of the principal reasons for writing this book is to let everyone know the truth about the Creator's existence: that He is a real being. As I have mentioned, I had the unique privilege and honor of meeting Him personally and want to share with you how I have learned over the years to communicate with Him and walk in His power. I also want to help you get connected, or reconnected, with the God of all Creation in an easy, fun, and exciting way that will bring more joy, happiness, and fulfillment into your life than you have ever experienced before. You can achieve this by learning the art of walking with God and how to invite His presence into your life.

You see, there are thousands of people out there with broken hearts and shattered dreams, living with crushed hopes that were never fulfilled. Time ran out for many of them as they grew old, and others just gave up along the way. For them, their dreams and plans never materialized or came to fruition. My grandfather was one of these people; he told me just before he died that he had lived his whole life without God's presence and only found Him and His power at the very end of his life, one year before he died. The Lord

God has promised you that He Himself will give you the desires of your heart and will help you to fulfill those dreams if you seek and follow Him: "Delight yourself also in the Lord, and He shall give you the desires of your heart" (Psalm 37:4 NKJV).

The next time you catch an airplane or ride a bus or take a train or just walk down the street, take a careful look all around. This is what you will see in the eyes of many decent people: regret, desperation, loneliness, anger, anxiety, despair, fear, and hopelessness. Many good, hardworking people tried doing it their way and only got so far in life. It doesn't have to be this way. Your heavenly Father has always been there for you, since the moment you were born, to help you through all your challenges and obstacles so you can get the most out of life.

But you need to understand that He will only draw near to you if you draw near to Him: "Draw near to God and He will draw near to you" (James 4:8 NKJV). He does not violate free will or invade your privacy (unless it's absolutely necessary). We are not His robots or drones or windup toys. He is patiently waiting on you to invite Him into your life. I have been living and walking in the power of the Almighty Creator for the past twenty years, and it's been the most amazing and wonderful experience. I have experienced what I like to call "mini miracles," or supernatural happenings, all around me consistently throughout my life.

I will share some of these stories in this book and show you how I was able to accomplish that. You see, as I have discovered, the Creator wants to be an integral part of everything you do, from the time you wake up until the time you go to bed at night. He wants to be at the center of your life, so He can help you, prepare you, and enable you to succeed in all your endeavors and dreams. He promises in His instruction manual (the Bible) to help you succeed and prosper you.

But more importantly, He wants to develop your character, because as you will find out, it will be His ability working through your availability that will help produce miraculous events along the way. It's a wonderful feeling knowing that He is with you and at your side and has your back at all times. But this incredible resource is not exactly free: It comes with a price. Part of that cost includes the sacrifice of your time, so you can devote yourself to Him by making a commitment to His principles and His ways.

> *For I know the plans I have for you," declares the Lord,*
> *"plans to prosper you and not to harm you, plans to*
> *give you hope and a future.*

— Jeremiah 29:11 (NIV)

If you are a chef, the Lord God wants to help you prepare new and creative healthy meals like never before, so you can become the best possible cook you can be in your area of influence and impress your boss and colleagues by bringing in new customers. If you're a schoolteacher, He wants to show you the best method to communicate lessons to your students in ways that will inspire and motivate them and prepare them for the future. If you are a student, you may need His help preparing for exams, getting through school, and obtaining your diploma or degree.

If you are in law enforcement, a firefighter, or first responder, He wants to keep you safe and show you the best way to save lives and help others in whatever situation you're confronted with. If you're a pilot, He would like to get you and your passengers to their destination safely and on time. This is true especially when there is a technical problem during the flight. If you're a doctor, nurse, or medical assistant, you may need His help in the surgery or operating room or just diagnosing what's wrong with the patient or deciding the best way to treat an individual. If you're a lawyer or legal assistant, you may need some help in the courtroom or preparing your case against a tough judge. If you are a movie director, you might need some help conveying the film's message in hopes of winning an Oscar and getting more creative ideas that will help generate increased ticket sales. If you are an engineer, you may need His help figuring out how to solve complex formulas to problems to get your job done more efficiently. If you are in the military, you could really use His help keeping yourself and your comrades alive, alert, and out of harm's way. If you are a preacher, ordained minister, or pastor, you will need His assistance to keep doing His special work.

And you need to know that your effort is not in vain, for I have personally met the Lord and can assure you, great is your reward. If you're an athlete, He can help enhance your natural abilities so that you stand out from the rest and start for your team by catching the eye of the head coach. If you're a waitress, with God's favor, you can end up making just as much in tips as you do with your regular salary. If you're a bus driver or train operator, stay-at-home mom or single parent, contractor, plumber, deli clerk, electrician, auto mechanic, garbage collector, dentist, accountant or financial analyst, janitor, actor, or author of a book, or whatever your profession, He is going to help you be the very best you can be in that occupation so that you stand out and shine. It does not really matter what you do for a living or what profession you are in (as long as it does not hurt anyone or break any laws). We all need Him to help us in our jobs, professions, and personal lives. This book was written for you and will help show you how to bring the Almighty Creator's power, creativity, and presence into your life, so you can be successful, healthy, and happy in all you accomplish.

I believe that everyone at some point in their life is searching for that special power to help them get to where they want to go and assist them in becoming what they desire to be. I have found that secret power and learned how to access it, and you can too. That mysterious power that everyone is searching for can be found within the pages of the Bible. The power of God will help you succeed in this life, and it's available to you. With His power, you can become the person you want to be, whether it is a musician or astronaut, singer or artist, entrepreneur or diplomat, or whatever else it is in life that you desire to be. It's God's power that will help you get there, and He will aid you in achieving and fulfilling that desire and dream, in accordance with His will. It's His promise to you.

This power will come to you when you learn how to walk with God and apply the principles within the pages of the Bible. Do all that you can do on your end and all that's within your control and influence, and then let God partner up with you to do everything that is outside of your control. The Creator, God, who is the author of the Bible, will make sure you meet all the right people and help connect you with all the individuals you need to make sure your dream is fulfilled.

> *It is impossible to rightly govern the world without God and the Bible.*
>
> —George Washington

Professor Chan and the Accounting Class

> *My help comes from the Lord, who made heaven and earth.*
>
> —Psalm 121:2 (NKJV)

About a week and half after I experienced my encounter with the Creator, I went to talk to my accounting instructor. I was not performing well in his class and was barely passing the exams, so I went to his office to drop the class; I was convinced that it was my only viable option. I figured I could always retake the class the next semester when I was more prepared and didn't have such a heavy workload and other classes to worry about. The spiritual encounter, I thought, was a wonderful experience, but I determined that that's all it really was. What I did not realize was what was going to happen next. I found Professor Chan in his office and asked if I could speak to him about dropping the class; I even had my drop slip in my hand. I explained to him that I was not doing well on the exams and was performing poorly.

He then looked at me rather curiously and said these words: "Something or someone spoke to me about you and told me that I am supposed to help you."

Professor Chan went on to say that I should not drop the class but hang in there, come to him for help during his office hours, and continue to turn in the homework assignments and extra credit work. What surprised me completely is when he stated that even if I failed the remaining exams, he would find a way to help me pass the class with a C grade at the very least, so I didn't have to worry about passing the class as long as I hung in there and just did my best.

It was at that moment that I immediately remembered the encounter with the Creator a week and a half earlier; I was stunned to realize that it was all not just a nice pleasant experience. I knew and understood that the Creator had spoken directly to Mr. Chan about me. Even if I didn't pass the remaining exams, Mr. Chan was going to find a way to pass me. Now, one thing to keep in mind is that college professors don't talk like that, especially a sharp and highly intelligent professor. He did things strictly by the book, a no-nonsense type of guy who never cuts corners. I was not only being asked to stick with the accounting class, I was also being encouraged not to give up. Wow. I thought he barely knew me.

When I showed up for class the following week, something else truly extraordinary and magical happened: The accounting material I was working on suddenly seemed very easy to comprehend and do. I'm not saying that I instantly knew how to do the whole book, but the material I was working on became easy to understand, almost as if the Creator had raised my IQ level when He touched me with His power, unblocking whatever was hindering me from learning. The accounting material now was as simple as a walk in the park on a sunny day. I ended up passing the class without any problem.

Professor Chan also took note of my performance and offered me an internship at his firm, so I could learn more about accounting, an offer I gladly accepted.

I began to realize at this point that God is very real and really wanted to help me. This was the beginning of my walk with the Lord God Almighty. I was experiencing my very first miracle, along with an answered prayer. This event changed my life forever.

The Scholarship

> *And you shall know the truth, and the truth shall make you free.*
>
> —John 8:32 (NKJV)

As I was wrapping up my final courses and remaining units at the City College of San Francisco to transfer to another school, I was approached by a friend who was attending Golden Gate University. We had studied together before transferring to other colleges and became good friends. He told me that the university he was attending was giving out scholarships for minority students and encouraged me to apply. It was called the Head Way Scholarship Program. For some reason, I didn't fill out the paperwork until the very last day it was due. I just kept procrastinating and putting it off, thinking it was all just a waste of time. I was just beginning to walk with God, and so I had little faith at the time. I was convinced they were never going to grant me a scholarship. I thought if I wanted to transfer to the university, I was going to have to get a student loan and work full time. Late that afternoon, something unusual prompted me to complete the essay and submit the application. So I got it done and dropped it off at the university and did not think much more about it.

A few weeks later, a young woman from the admission's office called and said she wanted to see me for an interview regarding the scholarship. I was really surprised by the call. We set up the day and time to meet. When I arrived at the interview, she asked me questions about my application, personal life, and employment status.

Then she asked me one final question that completely threw me off: "What is a motto or a saying that you live your life by?"

I honestly did not know what to say or how to respond to that question, so I asked her for a few seconds to think about it, which she granted. I quickly and silently prayed in my mind as she waited, *Heavenly Father and Lord Creator, who spoke to me the other day, please help me. What do I say?* I knew my answer could determine whether I get the scholarship or not. Instantly, the answer came to me from a passage I had just read in the Bible a few days earlier, and it was something I was learning to apply in my life: "And you shall know the truth, and the truth shall make you free" (John 8:32 NKJV).

Now, I'm not sure how that came to me, but it just did. It had to be the Lord, because I was stuck in a bind and didn't know how to respond. I just said the prayer and then, just as quickly, received the answer. I also remembered that this saying is written in large letters outside one of the buildings at the City College of San Francisco, and I mentioned this to the administrator.

She looked at me with a smile and said, "I really like your answer, Luis. I also want you to know that I am granting you a full scholarship to Golden Gate University. All you need to do is show up on time and maintain a 3.0 GPA."

I was so stunned that all I could say was "Thank you." Then I left the room and never saw her again. I went on to graduate with a bachelor's degree in general management, and several years later, I obtained my master's degree in business (MBA). I know now, many years later, beyond a shadow of a doubt, that the Creator had a hand in getting me to turn in the application at the last moment on the last day it was due and gave me the right thing to say in the interview;

that was the favor I needed from the administrator, so I could get that scholarship. I basically got a full scholarship by showing up, answering some basic questions, and quoting a scripture. You see, I really needed that break desperately, but I realized that it all began with my morning prayers and a commitment to a daily devotion to the Lord God Almighty.

Chapter 2

The Power of Prayer: The Eighth Wonder of the World

He shall call upon Me, and I will answer him; I will be
with him in trouble; I will deliver him and honor him.

—Psalm 91:15 (NKJV)

Now the Lord spoke to Jonah and commanded him to deliver a message to a great city called Nineveh because its sins had reached heaven. It was God's intention to save that city. But Jonah fled from the presence of the Lord and took a ship that was on its way to Tarshish. So the Lord sent a great wind and tempest into the sea, which almost broke that ship apart. The mariners on the ship were all afraid of dying, so they cast lots and then confronted Jonah, who was fast asleep at the bottom of the boat. Jonah told them, and it was determined, that this terrible storm was all happening because of him. Although the sailors tried rowing the ship back to shore, it was of no use; the tempest and storm was only getting worse. So they cast Jonah into the sea as he personally requested, and only then did the waters become calm. Now the Lord had prepared a great fish to swallow up Jonah, so he was in the belly of that fish hotel for three days and three nights (some speculate that the fish could have been a whale). Now Jonah was in some very serious trouble and in deep anguish at the bottom of the sea, freezing inside of a large fish with seaweed wrapped all around his head, and in his distress, he said this prayer:

> "Then Jonah prayed to the Lord his God from the fish's belly. And he said: 'I cried out to the Lord because of my affliction, and He answered me. Out of the belly of Sheol [Hell] I cried, and You heard my voice'" (Jonah 2:1–2 NKJV).

So the Lord heard the prayer and spoke to the fish, and it vomited Jonah onto the dry land. Jonah got his prayer answered, which got him out of that mess and saved his life, and he got a second chance and learned a valuable lesson in the process. That lesson is that it is always a good idea to obey and trust God.

We can see that God was with Jonah during the entire process, from the time he was asked to deliver a message to Nineveh, through the storms of life, and up till the time God set him free from inside the prison of the fish's belly. Jonah was no different from you and me; he had doubts, insecurities, and fears, and he made mistakes just like anyone else. When he got into trouble through running away from God, disobedience, and sinful behavior, God's mercy and love were there to show him the way back. We can all find ourselves in hot water from time to time, but the Lord is there to help us get through the challenges, no matter what the situation looks like. The Lord hears us from wherever we are in life, including the bottom of the ocean, where Jonah was trapped and imprisoned; He is ready and willing to give us a helping hand, out of the problem, but it begins with prayer.

I like to call prayer the eighth wonder of the world because it's how we communicate with the Creator, so He can then begin to communicate with us; it's also how we get our prayer requests answered, including how to get out of a bad situation. Prayer has the power to turn an ordinary day into an extraordinary day. Once you learn how to pray consistently, you can begin to unleash prayer's great potential and power in your life; with faith, patience, and practice, your circumstances will begin to change in an exceptional way that will surprise everyone around you.

You see, prayer is a sacred tool to help you get through your day, week, and even the seasons of your life by helping you navigate safely through your journey. When David, the shepherd boy, defeated Goliath, you need to understand that he prayed before he went into battle, and God's presence went with him; only then was he able to confidently handle the giant problem in the proper way. The God of heaven in time would then raise David up to become a great king and lead the nation of Israel. You see, prayer softens the battlefield, and He levels the playing field, so by the time you show up, things start running a lot smoother and easier for you at school or at work or wherever you are having problems.

But for prayer to work effectively, you need to do it regularly, and you need to be in the right relationship with the Lord, so He can begin to answer the prayers on your behalf. Please understand that God is not a genie in a bottle or some cosmic Santa Claus, ready to give you whatever you want. On the contrary; He is your heavenly Father and is there to guide you in life, so you can make the right choices along the way, so He can then give you what's best for you. Keep in mind that the Lord is more interested in developing your godly character than just giving you material possessions. He wants to develop your character so that when you do get the answers to prayer, you will have the discernment and maturity to manage the blessing He is going to send: otherwise, that big blessing may just slip right out of your hands.

The next several chapters will show you how to enable that relationship and how to gain God's favor in the process. One of the first ways to help usher His presence and power into your life is to develop a personal relationship with Him. You can do this by making a daily call to Him: "The Lord is near to all who call on him, to all who call on him in truth" (Psalm 145:18 NKJV). There are countless scriptures that begin with, "I call upon the name of the Lord." That call is not a phone call or a conference call. I am referring to prayer, or simply just talking to Him, and the best part is that it's free; it doesn't cost you a cent, and you don't even need a service provider. Your body is already built for wireless communication with your Creator. Isn't that wonderful? In other words, we don't have any excuse not to communicate with Him. It's a free service, and you can pray from wherever you are. It truly is one of the best gifts God has given us, and many people don't even realize how powerful it really is or take advantage of all its benefits. It is a great present from our heavenly Father.

But you may not have known this unless you have had a chance to read what I like to call *The Creator's Manual*, or the Bible. This is His book and His Word to all humankind. I talk more about this in the next chapter. For now, remember that all you need to do is start talking to the Lord each day, the way you would talk to your mom or dad, grandparents, or someone in authority that you love, respect, trust, and look up to. When you talk or pray, just do it normally and naturally. Be yourself: You're an original; there is no one on the earth quite like you. You don't need to use any fancy words or say repetitive phrases, unless you want to; just talk from the heart and be sincere. Keep it real. He understands where you are coming from and everything that is facing you and what you are going through or coming out of. He knows all about your challenges, goals, and situation and is there to help you through it all. The Lord knows every detail of your life, including the number of hairs on your head, and knows exactly where you live. He has your address and knows every language on the face of the earth. Don't underestimate Him for one moment.

> *And without faith it is impossible to please God,*
> *because anyone who comes to Him must believe that*
> *He exists and that He rewards those who earnestly*
> *seek Him.*

—Hebrews 11:6 (NIV)

The relationship with the Lord God your Creator begins the same way any intimate relationship begins: by spending quality time with that person. Spending fifteen minutes a day in prayer and devotion is great way to start. When you pray, you begin to receive power; it's that simple. It's like putting your phone in a power outlet on the wall to charge: The longer you stay connected, the more power you will receive. It's also like filling up your car with a full tank of fuel at a gas station for the journey ahead. The God of heaven begins to fill you with His divine power as you connect with Him and spend quality time with Him. But keep in mind: With more prayer, you will experience more of His power and presence in your life. A greater investment of your time will yield more of a reward. In other words, just like a lot of things in life, what you put into it is what you're going to get out of it. If you're serious about walking in the power of the Almighty Creator, and you should be, then I encourage you and challenge you today to make a daily call to your heavenly Father. Set aside a few minutes every day so you can spend some time communicating with Him and developing your relationship.

Daniel in the Bible is a fitting example of a person who had a great relationship with Him and had a steadfast commitment to prayer. The Bible records that Daniel prayed to God three times every day (Daniel 6:10) and continually trusted the Lord of heaven to be with him wherever he went. One day, Daniel was sent into a lion's den by the mischievous workings of his envious adversaries. Hungry lions were waiting for Daniel, wanting to kill him and eat him alive, but guess what? Daniel had nothing to fear because the Lord God, to whom he prayed three times a day, and whom he personally knew and walked with each day, went with him into that lion's den. Those ferocious lions did not have any power to do any harm to Daniel because a greater and higher power was with him.

This account is in the scriptures; you can read it for yourself and see how, with God's angel and the Lord's presence at Daniel's side, those big cats turned into friendly kitties. Daniel eventually was taken out of the lion's den by King Darius, and because of Daniel's innocence, his enemies were put in there in his place. The Bible states this, and the story ends with those lions, I presume, having a very good lunch (but it wasn't Daniel they ate).

The way God helped Daniel face that problem is the way He will help you face challenges you're confronted with. Now, speaking of commitment, your Creator is waiting to hear from you. Your prayers can be said at any time of the day or night, but I personally prefer to talk to Him in the morning, before I begin my day for school or work. Tell Him about your day and your plans and about all that's on your heart and mind. Trust me: He wants to hear from you. He is just waiting to hear from you and wants you to ask Him for His guidance and His help with your day, your dreams, and your plans. Your day will turn out much better if you start it out by calling upon His name. If you ask, you will receive; it's that simple, and then He will begin to pour out His divine Holy Spirit and power upon you and give you guidance and direction.

You see, praying daily like Daniel will get you connected to the Almighty God in a most extraordinary way. As you learn to discipline yourself and spend fifteen minutes a day with your heavenly Father, you will begin to experience His awesome and loving power surrounding you, leading you, and protecting you. Over time, He will begin to speak to you audibly and through other delivery methods, like visions and dreams, and you will begin to hear and recognize His voice. It's truly amazing; it's very real and quite supernatural.

But remember: It comes with a commitment of some of your time and obedience to His will and Word. If we can find the time to spend two hours each day watching television, being on the computer, reading a book, talking on the phone, or playing video games, then surely we can find fifteen minutes out of our busy schedule so we can make an investment in our spiritual growth and develop our relationship with Him. Over time, you will begin to experience the power of the Almighty overshadowing you and walking alongside of you, just as he did with Adam in the cool of the day in the Garden of Eden. However, it begins by first developing a relationship with Him and making that daily call.

Walking with God is similar to working out regularly or going to the gym three times a week. For instance, when you exercise Monday, Wednesday, and Friday for a couple of hours, you typically end up doing some stretching, walking, jogging, or running, whether on the road, on a track, or a treadmill. In one of these workout sessions, you might also jump on the spin bike, swim for an hour, use weights or exercise equipment, or use various other techniques, like interval training, which can include push-ups, jumping jacks, squats, and sit-ups. Everyone who works out knows it's important to be consistent, disciplined, and focused if you're to succeed; they also understand it's necessary to get plenty of rest and maintain a proper and healthy diet. The good news is that within three months, your hard work begins to pay off, and you really start seeing some measurable results. Your body becomes leaner, is stronger, and develops more muscle and definition. You look better, feel younger, are more attractive, and are generally healthier. If you have the discipline to work out regularly each week or can commit to some kind of hobby each week, like playing a musical instrument, it requires the same kind of a commitment level for you to learn how to walk with God. When you work out consistently and make that investment, you will reap the physical and mental health benefits associated with weekly exercise. In other words, spend time with God the same way you spend quality time doing the things you love, and you will experience His power and presence like never before.

The same kind of thing happens when you invest time with God. You reap benefits, not only on a physical level but on a spiritual level, as well. When you spend time each week in prayer and reading God's Word, the Bible, and a few minutes each day meditating on Him, working on developing your character, and attending a local house of worship, then in approximately three to six months depending on your commitment level with God's guidance, you'll start experiencing spiritual growth, finding positive rewards, and seeing measurable results. You'll feel physically, mentally, and spiritually stronger and healthier, and your mind will have more clarity and feel at peace, no matter what problem you face. You won't get discouraged, intimidated, or worried as easily. You're more compassionate, patient, and understanding, and you'll genuinely want to serve and help people.

When you begin to pray, things start to happen for you; your requests get answered, and events materialize for you more quickly because you are connected to the source of all life. You will also, over time, naturally end up developing a sixth sense and will know of future events before they happen and be tipped off of impending or dangerous situations. This will serve as an early-warning alert system for you. This is truly incredible and one of the best-kept secrets; the average person is unaware of this benefit. As I mentioned briefly, walking with God is similar to working out; when you develop that spiritual faith muscle and use it, you reap the benefits from of all the time spent in expanding your spirituality. What you put into it is what you get out of it, just like a lot of things in life, as you may have already figured out.

So I say to you: Ask and it will be given to you; seek and you will find; knock and it will be opened to you.

*For everyone who asks receives, and he who seeks finds,
and to him who knocks it will be opened.*

— Luke 11:9-10 (NKJV)

Another reason I call prayer the eighth wonder of the world is because just about all my prayers have been answered. I have also personally witnessed on many occasions miraculous things happening around me as a result of prayer. Some of these supernatural events are shared in this book at the end of each chapter. Some prayers took a little longer than others, but the Lord does promise to give you the desires of your heart in His time. This daily prayer and devotion over time will grant you access to heaven. I have often heard people say that when they tried praying once, nothing happened, so they gave up and never prayed again. How about just trying to pray consistently and daily, like Daniel and others did in the Bible until you get your breakthrough and your prayer is answered? What you may need to understand is that the power of prayer takes some time to cultivate, and there are some prerequisites that have to be in place first, like daily devotion and, most importantly, developing your godly character. If you pray just one time, it's highly likely you're not going to see any measurable results, but with a little patience, just like practicing playing a musical instrument, you will begin to experience the beautiful music and melodies of your answered prayers.

All prayers are definitely heard, I can assure you, but getting them answered may take some time, patience, and perseverance on your part. When you begin to pray daily and consistently, remember to pray for others as well, not just for yourself. The Lord is the potter, and we are the clay, so ask Him each day in prayer to mold you and make you into the person He wants you to be; then you will experience more of a rapid response and answers to prayers and requests.

What people may not realize is that God is not just two steps ahead of you: He is one thousand moves ahead of you. This is a good reason to trust Him and why He is also called the Alpha and the Omega, which is Latin for "the beginning and the end." You see, He already knows everything that is going to happen to you throughout your entire life. Your life story was written in His book long ago, before you were even born. He has already seen your life played out from start to finish. We are kind of like actors in a play, and He has already written the script and knows what's going to happen to you. This is one of the reasons He wants to be there with you as you go through your journey in life. He is the author and finisher of our faith. He wants your story to end well by making the right choices and decisions, but it all begins with prayer.

With God at your side, you will have a serious advantage in avoiding pitfalls, poor choices, foolish decisions, and dumb mistakes along the way. In other words, your life will become a less bumpy ride and therefore more enjoyable and satisfying. With the Lord at your side and through your prayer time, He will help you choose wisely who to marry, what friends to hang out with, what profession to choose, what job offer to take, what school to attend, and so on. You will still face trials and tests along the way, but you will understand that these challenges arise to help perfect your character by making you a better person. He will be there to see you through it all, and you will not only get to your destination safely, but you will get there looking good and unashamed for all to see. And when people ask how you achieved this or accomplished that or completed mission impossible, you can point them straight to Him and give Him all the credit or, as the Good Book says, all the glory.

Listening to God

> *Call to me and I will answer you and tell you great*
> *and unsearchable things you do not know.*

—Jeremiah 33:3 (NIV)

Now, listening to God is equally as important as praying to Him. I encourage you to spend a few minutes in silence, listening for God's voice, when you're done praying. Give Him a chance to speak to you; don't just say a prayer and rush off. Give Him a few minutes each time you pray; He may just want to say something special to you that day. Be patient. He will often speak to you while you're praying to Him or when you're done praying. He may also speak to you in the middle of your day as you go about your business, as He has done for me, but you need to be actively listening for His voice.

His voice in scripture is likened to a "still small voice" (1 Kings 19:12 NKJV) or a gentle whisper. I have experienced Him speaking to me countless times as a still small voice: I have also heard it like a commanding and loving whisper. It's always the same loving voice; it's not your conscience, and it will get your attention if you're listening. Now, He may not speak to you every time you pray, but He will speak to you occasionally, and it usually is unannounced and unexpected. It may surprise you the first couple of times it happens, but then you will get used to it. It's amazing and supernatural.

If you've never heard God speak to you and desire to hear His voice, then I encourage you to ask God in prayer to touch and anoint your ears, so you can begin to hear His voice so you can get the guidance and direction you need in your life. There is a good reason why we have two ears and one mouth; I believe we should be spending twice the amount of time listening as speaking. I think you would agree that you learn more when you're listening than when you're just talking all the time. Get into the habit of listening for

God's voice, but also keep in mind that He can also speak to you in a dream or vision; through a person, priest, ordained minister, or pastor; through a situation or circumstance; through an answered prayer; and through reading the Bible. He really is not limited on how He can speak to you, so it's important to be listening. However, the more you pray and spend time reading God's Word, the Bible, the faster you will begin to hear and recognize His voice.

"My sheep hear My voice, and I know them, and they follow me."

— John 10:27 (NKJV)

Here is an example of a man who audibly heard the Lord God speak to him; he listened carefully to the instructions, which changed his life forever. In the book of Acts, chapter 9, we see Saul (whose name would later be changed to Paul) headed for the city of Damascus. He was on his way to arrest the disciples of the Lord and anyone affiliated with them, but suddenly, on the road to Damascus, a light from heaven shone all around him.

> Saul fell to the ground and heard a voice saying to him, "Saul, Saul, why are you persecuting me?"
>
> Saul said, "Who are you, Lord?"
>
> Then the Lord said, "I am Jesus, whom you are persecuting. It is hard for you to kick against the goads."
>
> Saul, trembling and astonished, said, "Lord, what do you want me to do?"

Then the Lord said to him, "Arise and go into the city, and you will be told what you must do."

Now the men who journeyed with Saul stood speechless, hearing the voice but not seeing anyone. There are plenty of examples in the Bible of the Lord God speaking to His people in an audible voice to communicate something important to them. They just needed to be listening and ready to respond in the right way, like Paul. In fact, Paul, after hearing the Lord's voice and receiving this calling, would end up writing two-thirds of the New Testament.

Here is a short story of how God spoke to King Solomon in a dream.

At Gibeon the LORD appeared to Solomon in a dream by night; and God said, *"Ask! What shall I give you?"* And Solomon said: "You have shown great mercy to Your servant David my father, because he walked before You in truth, in righteousness, and in uprightness of heart with You; You have continued this great kindness for him, and You have given him a son to sit on his throne, as *it is* this day. Now, O LORD my God, You have made Your servant king instead of my father David, but I *am* a little child; I do not know *how* to go out or come in. And Your servant *is* in the midst of Your people whom You have chosen, a great people, too numerous to be numbered or counted. Therefore give to Your servant an understanding heart to judge Your people, that I may discern between good and evil. For who is able to judge this great people of Yours?"

The speech pleased the Lord, that Solomon had asked this thing. Then God said to him: "Because you have asked this thing, and have not asked long life for yourself, nor have asked riches for yourself, nor have asked the life of your enemies, but have asked for yourself understanding to discern justice, behold, I have done according to your words; see, I have given you a wise and understanding heart, so that there has not been anyone like you before you, nor shall any like you arise after you. And I have also given you what you have not asked: both riches and honor, so that there shall not be anyone like you among the kings all your days. So if you walk in My ways, to keep My statutes and My commandments, as your father David walked, then I will lengthen your days." Then Solomon awoke; and indeed it had been a dream. (1 Kings 3:5–15 NKJV)

I believe the Bible is the best gift God has ever given to man. All the good from the Savior of the world is communicated to us through this Book.

—Abraham Lincoln

A Day of Divine Provision and a Most Unusual Morning at the Train Station

Blessed be the Lord, Who daily loads us with benefits, The God of our salvation! Selah.

—Psalm 68:19 (NKJV)

I woke up one morning ready to go to work but then realized at the last minute that I had no money to get to the office. I thought to myself, *What did I do with my cash?* This had occurred before debit cards were popular. I was completely broke and somehow did not realize that I had misplaced and mismanaged my money.

I said to myself, *How am I going to get to work now?* I needed to catch the train to go into San Francisco from Oakland, where I was living at the time. I searched everywhere for some money but only found a handful of change. I grabbed the change as I left for the door and headed to the train station a little annoyed. I knew it wasn't going to be enough but took it with me any way.

I thought, *What am I going to do now? Call in sick? I can't do that.* I had some important things I had to finish at work, and I couldn't get a ride because everyone I knew personally lived out of the area. I figured I was just going to talk to the agent at the train station when I got there and ask if I could get free pass for the day. I could pay them later that day, if someone loaned me some money, or I could take care of it tomorrow on Friday, when I got paid. This was the plan, so I prayed quietly all the way from my house to the train station, which was about a fifteen-minute walk. Now I knew that I did not have enough money to get to work, but what I did have was faith and a personal relationship with my heavenly Father, so this gave me some confidence and comfort.

I prayed, *Lord God, I don't have enough money to catch the train to get to work; please forgive me for my stupidity and for foolishly mishandling my money. I am sorry. If You're listening up there, grant me loving favor with the station agent so they can give me a free ticket or a day pass, so I can get to work.* I prayed this all the way to the train station and trusted God to help me. When I got to the train station, I realized this problem just got worse because there was no agent on duty or at the booth. I wondered what I was going to do now, because the train was leaving in seven minutes, and I was not about to jump the terminal dressed in a nice suit and tie or go through the emergency exit without permission with security cameras on.

I began to put the little change that I did have into the ticket machine, hoping it would be enough, but as it turned out, it was not. So I prayed again, *Abba Father, what do I do now?* I stared at the ticket machine, feeling hopeless. Suddenly, something tapped my shoulder, and a gentle voice whispered to me and said, "Turn around." As I turned around, one of the terminals that provide access once you pay and insert your ticket had miraculously opened up for me right before my eyes. It was closed just a few moments before, but now it was wide open. I thought to myself, "No way that's possible. It's just opened up for me without a ticket."

This kind of reminded me of the story in the Bible where God parted the Red Sea, so His people could go through on dry ground and get out of Egypt in a hurry because an army was pursing them. They needed to get to their destination, the Promised Land.

I looked around in the terminal and saw that I was all alone at that point, but I knew that God was making a way for me to get to work. I was not about to miss my train, and I decided it was now or never, so I went right through that terminal that had just magically opened up for me. I said, "Thank you, Lord," as I went through the terminal and headed for the train, which was about to leave.

I figured I would talk with the station agent when I got to San Francisco about my situation and about what just happened because I knew I could not exit at the other end without a ticket. Now the train ride into the city took about twenty-five minutes, so I prayed again: *Heavenly Father, give me special favor with the agent in San Francisco. I will need it to get out of the train station.*

In the meantime, the Lord provided a seat for me in a train filled with passengers, even though I arrived last. I sat down and began to read my Bible, like I do each morning, to honor God; it's just a short devotion I do before I start my workday. When I reached my stop, I got off the train and rode the escalator up to the platform and then immediately realized two things. One of the terminals to exit the train station was wide open. And guess what else? There was no agent at the booth again.

Now I thought to myself, *What are the chances of that happening? I have taken the train hundreds of times and this has never happened, not like this.* Either this was an incredible, well-orchestrated coincidence or something supernatural was happening. I wasn't sure if that agent was on a bathroom break or attending to an emergency, but I didn't have the time to stick around and wait for them to show up. I had to get to work, so I went through the terminal that was wide open and did not look back.

I just said, *Thank you, Lord,* as I went through the terminal. *I will talk with the station agent when I get off work and pay for my ticket then.* I was able to make it to work right on time, as if nothing happened at all, although the whole thing seemed very unusual and peculiar to me.

At lunchtime, I decided to go for a walk, since I didn't have any money to buy anything to eat that day. I had asked a couple of coworkers for a few bucks, so I could get a sandwich for some lunch, but unfortunately, for some reason, nobody had any money that morning. This was probably because it was too early in the day and toward the end of the week, and payday wasn't until Friday, the following day. I had drunk the company's coffee all morning and was getting a headache from not eating anything all day. So I decided to go for a walk to get my mind off food and hunger pangs. I walked from Montgomery Street down to Powell Street, which is about a fifteen-minute walk. I was just window shopping, and I prayed to the Lord about three times along the way to please provide lunch for me if it was possible. But nothing seemed to happen, and I wasn't even sure if He was listening to my prayer, with all these people walking in front of me. My headache was really starting to bother me, and so was my stomach because I was hungry and had worked hard all morning.

As I entered a store to look around, I just happen to run into this lovely girl I recently met and really liked.

She said to me, "Hi Luis, how are you? What are you doing down here?"

I told her that I worked in the area and that I was on my lunch break. She then asked me if I wanted to go to lunch with her, but since I was dead broke, I told her, "No that's okay. I am not really hungry."

The truth was, I felt like I was starving, but I was too embarrassed to tell her because even though I didn't know her well, I liked her a lot. As I was getting ready to walk away, she pleaded with me and insisted three or four times to please go to lunch with her.

"I could use the company, Luis. I will treat you. Come on," she said in her sweet voice.

I knew at that moment that the Lord was providing lunch for me, the same way He had provided the train ride for me. I figured, at that point, the best thing to do was accept her offer; it was now or never. I just had to humble myself, swallow my pride, and graciously receive God's provision and blessing through this person. She took me to a café close by and ordered me a fat burger with french fries, a fruit salad, and a drink. I was so stuffed when lunch was over that I thanked her and the Lord all the way back to the office. Can you imagine that?

This beautiful girl who bought me lunch that day reminded me of Queen Esther in the Bible, who was raised up for a special purpose and was placed in a certain position and at just the right time, so she could render aid and assistance to help God's people in a time of need. I also should note that I repented and asked the Lord to forgive me for telling her that I wasn't hungry when in reality I was. By this point, my confidence level in God's provision was high, so I didn't even bother to think about how I was going to get home. I knew from the way this day was going that all would be taken care of and provided for me, so I just left that matter in God's hands and didn't worry about it.

I was kind of hoping that the Lord would send a taxi or limo to pick me up and take me home, but it didn't quite happen that way. When I got back to the office, someone I spoke to from earlier in the morning unexpectedly came up to me and loaned me some money.

I said, "Thank you, Lord." I was able to use this money to get home and planned to use the money to pay for the train ride I had taken in the morning. By the way, the station agent didn't want my money after all and just told me thanks for letting him know.

I would like to point out something important: When you are at your lowest point and in your darkest hour, if you're willing to call upon the name of the Lord and just trust Him through whatever the situation is, that's when God will show up strong and mighty in your life and help you get through any challenge. You just need to find the time to invite Him into your life and then learn how to walk with Him each day, so you can partake in all his blessings and benefits.

Where Is the Lord?

In my distress I cried to the Lord, and He heard me.

—Psalm 120:1 (NKJV)

One night, I was coming home late from school. It was about ten o'clock, and I was very tired because it had been a long day, and it was dark and cold outside. I had to walk about ten blocks to my home because my car was not working properly, so I had been taking the bus to school and work. As I walked up the block, I was complaining the whole way to God about a recent breakup I had with a girl I was dating. I was heartbroken over the entire thing and was complaining to God about it. I instinctually knew that the Creator did not like my complaining, but I just kept going on, hoping He would do something about it. I was about three blocks away from my home when I reached the corner of the street. Suddenly, a large man about five feet ten and around 240 pounds, about twice my size and weight, came out of the shadows and took a big swing at me.

All I remember was seeing a huge fist coming straight at me, and fast. I heard a still small voice tell me to duck, and I did. The man missed my face by a fraction of an inch but managed to hit my backpack, causing all my books to go flying into the middle of street. I was in some serious trouble; I didn't even know this guy or why he was doing this. I was all alone, and to make matters worse, there was a car about ten feet in front of me, which had just pulled up with about three or four more of these hostile-looking thugs, and I should note that they were smiling and grinning.

I stepped back and whispered, "Where is the Lord? Heavenly Father, I am trouble; please help me." In a moment of crisis, you feel that there is no God who can save you because it's all happening so fast, and it feels so surreal. But you need to remember that feeling of being abandoned is only an illusion: "God is our refuge and strength, a very present help in trouble" (Psalm 46:1 KJV). Now this gangster thug did not hear me when I said, "Where is the Lord?" As I was thinking about what was going to happen to me, I noticed the facial expression of this man suddenly began to change. His face went from confidant and domineering and in total control of this situation, to worried, troubled, and terrified, all within about two or three seconds of me saying, "Where is the Lord?"

In fact, he looked completely frightened and not at all in control of this situation anymore. This thug's face went from "I gotcha" (with an evil grin) to an expression of complete surprise, like, "Oh, no, this cannot be possible," as if a ten-foot angel were standing behind me. This happened within seconds of me calling upon the name of the Lord, and this gangster did not take one more step toward me. In fact, he raced back to the car where his buddies were waiting for him, running as though his life depended on it. They sped off so fast and just left me there. I was just standing there with my books scattered in the middle of the street, wondering what had just happened and why they left so abruptly. You see, I was literally outgunned, outflanked, and outnumbered, so there was no logical reason for them to run away.

Then I realized that the Lord of hosts, as God is also called, must have shown up and spoken to these thugs in the same way He speaks to me in an audible voice; that's all I could rationally conclude. Now, just for the record, you need to know honestly that I did not see any angels or lights, or even hear anything. All I saw was his facial expression completely change from confidant to fearful in a matter of seconds, and he didn't take one more step near me after I called upon the name of the Lord. Psalm 55:16 (NKJV) says, "As for me, I will call upon God, and the Lord shall save me."

What I suspect may have happened was that the Lord, or one of His angels (whom I could not see), showed up in a nanosecond and spoke to him the way He speaks to me or perhaps showed him a vision that frightened him: "The Angel of the Lord encamps all around those who fear Him, and delivers them" (Psalm 34:7 NKJV). It usually is the case that these types of encounters with the Lord, the King of angels, are alarming; when He speaks to you in an audible voice, it catches you off guard, especially the first few times.

I am now going to give you a cleaned-up, censored version of what I imagine the conversation may have been like. Again, this is just my opinion, based on past experience. The message he may have received or vision he may have seen probably went something like this:

(To the man who had just attempted to assault me) "If you take one more step near my child and try to harm him in any way, this night is not going to end well for you and your friends."

If the thug did receive a message or vision, it may have seriously freaked him out, and that caused him to flee from me. Now, I am more than certain that whatever message he received from the Lord my Protector was most likely a lot more convincing, persuasive, and menacing than my clean and censored version in this book. You see, the Lord is there to protect you: "The Lord is my rock, my fortress, and my savior; my God is my rock, in whom I find protection. He is my shield, the power that saves me, and my place of safety (Psalm 18:2 NLT). It's His promise, and it's in His Word. He is your protector; you just need to be walking in His power and spend time with Him each day to receive that benefit. I will leave what the Lord may have really said to him or showed him up to your imagination, but whatever it was, it definitely worked, and he got the message in real time. He fled the scene almost like his very life depended on it.

As I picked up my books off the street and headed home, I realized a few things. First, the Lord got me to stop complaining about the breakup with the girl because He just delivered me from a very dangerous situation. The next insight I received was that the Creator was not only there to protect me from danger and hostile strangers, but He was showing me through this experience that He was also protecting me from an unhealthy relationship: This girl was going to ruin my life in the long run, and I knew, from her previous actions, that she wasn't God's choice or best for my life and future. She had all the bells and whistles that I wanted, but she did not have a godly character, and honestly, I was too immature and insecure at the time to properly manage a relationship. These qualities need to be in place and intact if a relationship is going to work, and it's especially important for a long-term commitment and marriage.

Chapter 3

The Power of a Daily Devotional: The Manufacturer's Manual

> *Study to show thyself approved unto God, a workman*
> *who needeth not to be ashamed, rightly dividing the*
> *word of truth.*

—2 Timothy 2:15 (KJ21)

Once you have learned the importance of praying daily, you can begin to spend a few minutes each day, or at least a couple of days a week, reading and learning more about what I like to call *The Creator's Manual*, which is the Bible. I have heard it said that praying is us talking to God, but reading the Bible, God's Word, is Him talking to us. The second way we can begin to walk in the power of the Almighty Creator is through daily devotion, or the reading of His Word. The Bible is not just a book for religious people, as the world would have you believe. On the contrary, it's a survival handbook for everyone who is born on the Creator's earth. It is commonly said that knowledge is power, especially when that knowledge is put into practical use and implemented. The Almighty states in His instruction manual, "My people are destroyed because of a lack of knowledge." Knowledge is very important and can be empowering because it helps you to be better informed; this will aid you in making the best decision and moral choice along the way. Another verse I like is Psalm 119:105 (NKJV): *"Your word is a lamp to my feet, and a light to my path."*

Therefore, it is critical to get familiar with the basic teachings and instruction of this manual. This Bible is like a manufacturer's manual; it teaches you many things, such as activating your faith, establishing your morality, and acquiring patience so you can get through your toughest challenges while avoiding the pitfalls in this world. This instruction manual was written to enlighten you about the fact that the Creator, the Lord God, does exist, and that He is a resource for everyone who seeks Him and wants His help and guidance. This manual was written by godly people over many centuries, scribes chosen by God Himself, who were inspired by His Spirit and presence to write the book for us. He did not just want to leave us here without basic instructions or without a guide to help us along the way because He knew that the world He created for us would not be easy at times, and there would be obstacles and challenges along the way.

My people are destroyed for lack of knowledge.

— Hosea 4:6 (NKJV)

When you purchase an iPhone or an iPad, a desktop/laptop computer, a flat screen TV, or whatever product it may be, it comes with a manufacturer's manual and some form of guarantee. The manufacturer's manual is typically a book that comes with your product; it can also come online to download. The manual, as you know, is designed to help you learn how to use all the item's features, so you can take advantage of all the benefits and get the most out of the product. Now, please understand that you are God's creation, His special design, made after His own image and likeness. He has left us a manual, so we can learn how to make moral choices and navigate safely through our journey in life and take advantage of all His benefits, so we can get the most out of life. When you begin to spend quality time reading God's Word, the Bible, the Creator will begin to pour out his Holy Spirit on you, and He guarantees it in this manual.

For me, His power is likened to a force field of energy all around me, and I experience an overwhelming spiritual presence that helps me navigate each day, week, and season of my life. When you begin to read his instruction manual regularly, you too will begin to feel His power flowing through you; this divine force helps you to feel uplifted and inspired in almost any situation. You also become encouraged and motivated to succeed in any good endeavor you set your heart and mind to. It's truly extraordinary and supernatural.

> *Wisdom is the principal thing; therefore get wisdom.*
> *And in all your getting, get understanding.*
>
> — *Proverbs 4:7 (NKJV)*

You can get yourself a *Creator's Manual* (the Bible) for the price of a meal at a fast-food restaurant, or you can go online and read it for free. There really is no excuse not to have a copy. I want to challenge you to spend fifteen minutes a day, or least a couple of times during the week, reading this instruction manual to make an investment in your spiritual awakening and development. You will be glad you did. As you read His Word each day, you will not only get insight into the internal workings of life and its mysteries but will begin to see the world through a God-like perspective, or as I like to call it, a new set of lenses.

When you spend quality time reading this Holy Book, you begin to experience an unseen presence, filling and encompassing you with divine power. When you read His Word, you're honoring Him with your life; the Lord God finds this pleasing. As a direct result of your devotion to Him, He will give you the solutions to problems and provide the answers you need in every situation and area of concern in your life. He will honor you because you have honored Him, and He will bless you with unprecedented favor wherever you go.

This is one of the best-kept secrets of the Bible, and the secular world is unaware of this hidden truth. There are times when this force field of light energy and this spiritual power is so strong upon me that I feel sometimes like a Jedi knight right out of the *Star Wars* movies. Let me explain to you what this force feels like and what it can look like: Oftentimes, people who don't even know you will begin to open doors for you as you walk into buildings, offices, and supermarkets, just out of courtesy to you, motivated by a loving spirit. People will tend to give you discounts, breaks, and preferential treatment wherever you go.

This doesn't necessarily happen every day, but it will occur on a regular basis. You will kind of feel like a celebrity, but you need to stay very humble because the Lord God Almighty does not like arrogance or excessive pride. We are no better than anybody else just because God's power has a softening effect on people to do special things or favors for us. At restaurants, the staff will frequently do their best to get you in quickly and offer you the best possible seat with a nice view, regardless of your race, color, or social status. You will often be treated like royalty or like someone very special.

At your place of employment, your boss will give you a raise or ask you to take on a special assignment or consider you for a promotion sooner than expected. But remember, this will happen when it's the right time and season. My all-time favorite is that I usually get parking for my car wherever I go, regardless of the heavy traffic and the completely full parking lot. It's God's favor being provided for you; it is not luck or magic, and it's amazing and supernatural.

These are just a few benefits I have personally experienced, but there are many more. People have called me Lucky Luis many times over the years, but it's not luck at all; it's the favor of the Most High God on me, and it can encompass you, as well. It all begins with prayer and devotion. The science behind this is simply that the presence of the Almighty Creator is walking with you, and as a result, you will be honored and treated well wherever you go because He is the Lord of all the earth, and His divine presence is with you wherever you go: "For the Lord your God is with you wherever you go" (Joshua 1:9 NKJV).

Reading the Bible will also teach you how to pray and how to approach the Lord, so you can get your prayers answered. We can begin to walk in the power of the Almighty God by being obedient to His Word, commands, and instructions. The various stories and lessons we learn from His Word, the Bible, will help us become compassionate people and will also help us develop our godly character, which is what our Creator desires the most. Because of your steadfast commitment and devotion to Him and His principles, you will, over time, be given unusual wisdom, understanding, insight, and revelation, not only about God but also about the world around you.

As you read His Word each day, His power and Holy Spirit will be poured upon you. This will help you walk and live in a new way, and you will begin to see the right solution to whatever problems you are facing. This will happen by way of new perspectives presented to you by angels or other supernatural forces, and this phenomenon will help you tremendously both at work and in your personal life. Developing a godly character or a Christlike character is one of the main goals of reading the Bible. This manual is there to provide instruction and guidance, so we can move toward a better, safer, and healthier lifestyle.

Reading His Word regularly will help you activate the process of living His Word and then becoming like His Word. It is then that you will experience walking in His power and authority. Challenge yourself to spend fifteen minutes in His instruction manual each day, and you will begin to experience His power and presence like never before. As you acquire this habit of reading the Bible daily, you will soon discover that it is not a chore or duty but is something to look forward to, and you will begin to savor this time with your Creator.

> *I have a fundamental belief in the Bible as the Word of God, written by those who were inspired. I study the Bible daily.*
>
> —Sir Isaac Newton

The Daily Bread

> *All Scripture is God-breathed and is useful for teaching, rebuking, correcting and training in righteousness, so that the servant of God may be thoroughly equipped for every good work.*
>
> —2 Timothy 3:16–17 (NIV)

One day, I decided to start an email scripture reading. I asked for help with this from a colleague, and I invited coworkers who expressed interest and indicated they would like to be added to the list. We knew that there were several people at work who attended various churches in the area, and because we had a common connection and interest in our own personal spiritual growth and development, we wanted to encourage each other. We figured it would help us get through the week at work while helping us stay in touch. There was already a member's list in place for this Daily Bread email; however, the reading was not being sent out consistently. The Daily Bread was simply one scripture or passage out of the Bible, sent once a day, for the purpose of encouraging us through our busy work day. It was just an uplifting message intended to help everyone begin every day with a positive attitude and a good frame of mind. It only took about three minutes to send it out each day, and it was not big deal. But before we were going to send it out every day, I wanted to make sure that everyone on the existing list was still okay with it. I did not want to offend or annoy or upset anyone, so I let everyone know that starting the following week, we would begin sending out the Daily Bread email every day. I asked anyone who did not want to participate to please let me know so we could have them removed. At the time, we had about twenty-eight people on the list.

To my great surprise, shortly after I sent out my introductory email, I began receiving daily requests to have people removed from the list. By the end of the week, we had lost well over half the names on the list. This was exactly the opposite of what I thought would happen. I was shocked, to say the least, and was very discouraged. I asked myself how so many people who claimed they loved God and wanted to know Him better, now wanted to be removed from a daily scripture reading that was free of charge and being provided to encourage them and uplift their spirits.

On my lunch hour, I sat at a bench all alone, just staring at the concrete floor in disbelief. I was heartbroken and disappointed. I will never forget that day. I was feeling like I just went through a breakup and could not even eat my lunch. I asked the Lord, "How is it possible that almost half of the people on our Daily Bread list are gone, and we are just getting started?" I could understand losing two or three people, but not 50 percent of the list; come on. I took it hard because it was my idea, and I just sat there completely dismayed for almost an hour. While I was looking down at the floor and feeling broken-hearted, suddenly, the Lord spoke to me and said, "Do not feel brokenhearted or discouraged, for they have not rejected you but have rejected Me," and then He revealed to me that He was separating the wheat from the chaff, otherwise known as weeds. Wow. All of a sudden, I felt better and knew everything was going to turn out all right. I lifted my head up and was able to eat my lunch.

I was reminded that this was not necessarily about me or my idea, but about their personal relationship and walk with Him, the Lord.

This story has a happy ending, because over the next few weeks, a flood of new people found out about the new daily reading and asked to be put on the Daily Bread list. It was literally a two-for-one. For every person who asked to be dropped from the list, the Lord sent me two more to be added. Within ninety days, we had more people on the list than we originally started with, and the list continued to grow from that point on. I was amazed at and greatly encouraged by the power of God. As for those folks who asked to be dropped from this list, I gracefully granted them their request. I should also mention that to this day, those people don't even have a clue that the Lord spoke to me about them, and I never bothered to tell them, either; I just prayed for them and moved on. As far as I can remember, there were well over a hundred names on the Daily Bread list when I left the firm. This all was possible because I had learned how to walk in the power of the Almighty Creator.

The Police Officer

Call upon me in the day of trouble; I will deliver you,
and you shall glorify Me.

—Psalm 50:15 (NKJV)

One night, an attorney asked me to work late. At the time, I was corporate securities paralegal at a law office in Silicon Valley, and honestly, I was a little annoyed at the request because 5:30 p.m. was the end of my work day, and I just really wanted to go home. However, I knew that this particular client and his situation were very important to the attorney, so I opted to stay and get the work done. She promised to give me a ride, so I could catch the 8 p.m. commuter train home. When we were done working at the office, we got into her BMW and began the drive to the train station a few blocks away. She was in a hurry to get me there on time, so I would not miss my train. Suddenly, a police officer turned on the siren and flashing lights directly behind us. Apparently, in her rush to get me to the train station on time, she ran a stop sign. We had both been talking, and because it was dark out, we did not realize that we ran the stop sign.

She pulled over and became very nervous. I don't think she had ever had a moving violation ticket up to this point because she appeared very worried. As the police officer started walking toward her car, I was prompted by the Lord to pray for her, because she was a nervous wreck and could not even speak straight because her voice quavered so much.

I prayed right in front of her and said out loud, "Heavenly Father, I pray in the mighty name of Jesus that she will not get a ticket today because of me. Please give her unprecedented favor with the police officer, if it's according to your will. Amen."

It was a very fast prayer, and as I said, "Amen," I received an instant reply from the Lord God: "Tell her not to worry or to be afraid, for she will not be getting a ticket tonight." I told her that the Lord just spoke to me and said that she would not be getting a ticket tonight, so she was not to worry about the police officer.

"Just trust the Lord now," I said.

She looked at me like I was crazy and had just lost my mind by making such a bold statement while the police lights were flashing in the rearview mirror. Now, you need to know that when the Lord speaks to you, your confidence level will skyrocket to 100 percent, so you yourself are convinced that the words you just received are going to happen, no matter what. There is no doubt in your heart that this is definitely going to happen. That's one way to know that it's the Lord speaking to you.

By this time, the officer had approached the window. He looked serious and appeared to be the type of guy who wouldn't bend any rules or give you any breaks. In a commanding voice, he said,

"Are you aware that you ran a stop sign?" He then asked for her identification.

She was so scared that she had trouble answering the simple question but managed to tell him that she was sorry and that all she was trying to do was get me to the train station on time. In her panic, she forgot my name and called me her "worker," which I found amusing. The next thing the officer said may have completely surprised the attorney, but not necessarily me.

The officer said, "You know, something or someone just spoke to me about you, and all of a sudden, I don't feel like giving you a ticket."

The officer also said that I could leave so that I didn't miss my train; I reminded the attorney that everything was going be all right, and she was not to worry, and said, "Have a good night," and I left.

I did not know what specifically happened until the next morning when I arrived at the office. She told me that the police officer did not give her a ticket after all but only a warning. I told her that was great and also reminded her that when I prayed, the Lord spoke to me and told me to tell her that she would not be getting a ticket. The lesson here was that we just need to trust Him at all times when He speaks to us.

I will also add that from that day forward, the attorney began treating me a lot differently. She was much nicer to me and had a newfound respect for me. I enjoyed her change of heart because she had been very tough on me up to that point. I believe that she may have been a little spooked or shaken up by the whole thing and realized in the end that I definitely had some kind of a relationship and divine connection with God.

Chapter 4

The Power of Meditation: Perfect Peace and the Mind of Christ

Oh, how I love your law! I meditate on it all day long.

—Psalm 119:97 (NIV)

King David would often meditate at night on the greatness of God, and he would recite or sing the Psalms; I have listed two of them here for your reference. At the end of some of the verses you will see the word *Selah*. It indicates a pause for contemplation, meditation, and reflection: "Tremble, and do not sin; meditate in your heart upon your bed, and be still. Selah" (Psalm 4:4 NASB). When David the shepherd boy was asked how he would defeat Goliath, he told the king and his officials that the Lord who delivered him (David) from the paw of the bear and the paw of the lion would also deliver him from the ten-foot-tall giant Philistine warrior. David reflected and meditated on past victories that the Lord had given him. This encouraged him greatly, and he was then confident and mentally at peace, knowing that God would help him with the giant, and in the end, it all turned out well for David, partly due to the power of meditation.

For "who has known the mind of the Lord that he may instruct Him?" But we have the mind of Christ.

— 1 Corinthians 2:16 (NKJV)

I am going to share a little secret with you: This may be hard to believe, but it's the truth, and as God is my witness, I honestly don't recall the last time I had a bad day because it's been so long I can't even remember. But that was not always the case. I used to have a good day once in a blue moon, and a bad day just about every week, but once I learned the meditation technique I found in the Bible, all that changed. What I began to do was to apply this biblical principle, and after I practiced it a little, I found myself on the way to a healthier state of mind, and most importantly, I was at peace. As a young man, I frequently was depressed and unhappy. This state of mind was obvious to others, and it almost always drove people and relationships away. I could not figure it out, and I was constantly feeling down, angry, and disappointed. I was not aware at the time how powerful thoughts are and how they can affect one's mood and attitude. I began to realize, after I read the Bible, that my thoughts were actually controlling and affecting my mood. Having sad, bad, angry, and unhappy thoughts every day was just bringing me down. Since I was having a lot of negative and unhealthy thoughts, I was constantly feeling discouraged. I was unaware for a long time what was causing my depression.

Then one day, during my daily devotion time, I asked the Lord in prayer, as I always do, to please illuminate my understanding. As I studied the word of God, I came across the following passage: "Whatever is true, whatever is noble, whatever is right, whatever is pure, whatever is lovely, whatever is admirable, if anything is excellent or praiseworthy think about such things. Whatever you have learned or received or heard from me, seen in me-put it into practice. And the God of peace will be with you" (Philippians 4:8-9 NIV). That was it; I had an instant revelation and saw the light. I needed to start changing the channel in my mind and in my thinking. I began practicing positive thinking and embracing healthy thoughts. I left no room for negativity. I started thinking only about—and I really mean *only* about—things that were true, noble, right, pure, lovely, admirable, and positive, just like the scripture said. There would be no more room for depressing, disappointing, or angry thoughts. Those days were over and done with. I would intentionally refuse to think about anything negative and instead only allow healthy and positive thoughts into my mind. I created for myself a filtering process, so I could focus only on the good and uplifting thoughts.

> *And do not be conformed to this world, but be transformed by the renewing of your mind, that you may prove what is that good and acceptable and perfect will of God.*

> — Romans 12:2 (NKJV)

I have learned through the word of God to manage my thought life in a positive and constructive way and not let random negative thoughts manage me. I am not going down that road of sorrow again; I was held captive there long enough and in bondage to that mind-set for many years, until God's Word set me free. There is no room now in my mind for negative thinking or unhappy thoughts concerning the past or present. This is due primarily to the power of meditation. Just meditating on Him will fill you with his power, presence, and peace.

Also, I don't live in the past, reflecting on any disappointments, breakups, or hurts I've experienced along the way. I instead reminisce on good times and focus on the lessons I learned from each experience. The God of heaven doesn't want you living in the past, either. The Lord wants you living in the present and in a healthy state of mind. Each day truly is a gift; that's one reason why it's called the present. I have learned how to forgive others and myself, and not hold grudges against anyone for any reason. I don't walk in any kind of unforgiveness anymore. Whatever anyone did to me in the past was no longer my worry or concern; I just turned it over to God and let it go. I have learned to let go and let God have His way, and I feel a lot happier, healthier, and stronger. I am not chained to anyone from my past because I have learned to forgive them and move on. All my thoughts now are positive, healthy, and uplifting ones, and these are the only ones I allow in my mind.

Now when I do get some bad news, I do the best I can to solve the problem quickly while keeping my mind on God, knowing and trusting that He will help me resolve it and get through it. But I caution you, please don't fall into the trap of dwelling on the problem all day. They say that worrying is wasted energy, and it really is. I don't worry that much anymore about anything. What I do instead is trust God to help me work out the solution.

For example, the only time I think about my bills is the moment I am about to pay them. Fear and anxiety can be paralyzing, but keeping your mind consistently on God, which is a form of meditation, will neutralize and counteract those unpleasant emotions. My mailman once told me that he has several homes he goes to where people only pick up their mail once a month. When I asked him how come, he said they told him that they live in fear of what might be coming in the mail. I have learned, through this art of meditation, to face fear quickly so it does not get a chance to take root and grow into anxiety and paralyze me against taking action.

I often quote the following scripture out loud and meditate on this passage when I am faced with troubling news: "Whenever I am afraid, I will trust in You" (Psalm 56:3 NKJV). My foster mother Anita is eighty-five years old; she gave me some good advice long ago, and I am going to share it with you. She said to stop inventing things to worry about. If you really think about it, she's right because a lot of the things we worry about never materialize. The Bible says in Isaiah 26:3 (NKJV), "You will keep him in perfect peace, whose mind is stayed on You, because he trusts You." This is one of the reasons why meditation is very important to God, and it should be to you. Keeping your mind fixed on God will help keep you balanced and in perfect mental peace; all it takes is just a little bit of patience and practice.

You can meditate with your eyes closed or open. A good technique I recommend is to close your eyes for about ten minutes each day and focus on a passage of the Bible and a peaceful and tranquil thought about God. Keep repeating the passage as you slowly breathe in and out. Give your body a chance to relax and to focus on your Creator. You will begin to feel better in just a few minutes.

Another key thing to remember is to keep your mind on your heavenly Father throughout the day as you go about your business: keep your mind on His promises and on His Word. This will help you to not get sidetracked and fall into depression or negative thinking. Meditation is a powerful tool to help you stay mentally focused, spiritually strong, and physically healthy. Once you get the technique down, which takes only about two weeks, you won't need any antidepressants or anxiety pills to keep you mentally sane, stable, and balanced. You see, there were no pharmaceutical companies around in biblical days, so this is one of the techniques our ancestors used, and it's one of the best-kept secrets. This is one of the methods our past relatives used to take care of depression, fear, and anxiety. They did not need medications for depression. They just applied this simple biblical principal and technique and then trusted in the Lord.

Now, please be practical. It does not hurt to get some rest or recreation, eat healthy, and get some exercise. This will also help you develop a positive outlook. In some cases, your condition may be critical and severe enough, so you should consult with your doctor; however, for the majority of the time, God's formula can work wonders. One of the keys is to do all things in moderation and remember to maintain a healthy balance between work and play. Believe it or not, the Lord God also wants you to have some fun in your life, so you can rest and relax and enjoy yourself.

Blessed is the man who walks not in the counsel of the ungodly, nor stands in the path of sinners, nor sits in the seat of scornful; but his delight is in the law of the Lord, and in His law he meditates day and night. He shall be like a tree planted by the rivers of water, that brings forth its fruit in its season, whose leaf does not wither; and whatever he does shall prosper.

— Psalm 1:1–3 (NKJV)

Meditation is good for your mental and physical health; it keeps you physiologically balanced. You won't freak out over every little thing that comes up. Meditating regularly on Him, His promises, and His Word will definitely help you lower your anxiety and stress level; it may even help lower your blood pressure because you are relaxing and trusting in Him and not worrying as much. Meditating on all the blessings that you do have is an effective way to help you stay mentally balanced and fit. In other words, whenever you are feeling discouraged, take a few minutes to count all the blessings that you have. Now, if you follow the Lord's advice in his instruction manual, the Bible, then you too may end up saying one day, "You know, God was right all along. This meditation stuff He talked about really works. I honestly cannot remember the last time I had a bad day; it's been so long, I just can't seem to remember."

This Book of the Law shall not depart from your mouth, but you shall meditate in it day and night, that you may observe to do according to all that is written in it. For then you will make your way prosperous, and then you will have success.

— Joshua 1:8 (NKJV)

I have an interesting story to share. One day, while I was an undergrad student working on my bachelor's degree, I was approached by one of my professors. This man was my operations management instructor. He also just happened to be the head of the executive MBA program at the university I was attending. He asked me to meet with him in his office for a few minutes, but he didn't say why. When I came to his office, he told me that he had never met a student quite like me before, a person who was always in a pleasant mood.

He said, "Luis, you are always in a good mood, relaxed and happy. I have never seen you upset, worried, or troubled about anything throughout the semester. Do you ever get depressed? What's your secret?"

I told him, "It's a technique I learned in the Bible."

I quoted him Philippians 4:8-9 (NIV): "Whatever is true, whatever is noble, whatever is right, whatever is pure, whatever is lovely, whatever is admirable - if anything is excellent or praiseworthy - think about such things. Whatever you have learned or received or heard from me, or seen in me - put it into practice. And the God of peace will be with you." I also shared with him just about everything else I've mentioned in this chapter.

He looked at me rather curiously and said, "Thank you for sharing this information; I do find it very interesting."

Now, I'm not sure if he ever used this meditation technique, but my mental stability and calmness certainly did get his attention above all the students and was notable enough to get me a personal meeting with him.

> *Within the covers of the Bible are the answers for all the problems men face.*
>
> —Ronald Reagan

The Landlord

*Do not be deceived, God is not mocked; for whatever
a man sows, that will he also reap.*

—Galatians 6:7 (NKJV)

For a couple of years, I rented a two-bedroom apartment in
northern California. The landlord was always very friendly to me
and would regularly chat with me because we got along well. He
would bring up conversations about the weather, current events,
politics, and sports whenever he and I met up. As I came to find out
over the course of the years, he had a reputation for not returning
security deposits when tenants moved out. Some of these cases, I
presume, were legitimate, but I believe several were questionable. I
was told by previous tenants that he would look for any reason to
deduct a portion of the deposit or just not refund anything at all.

The time came when I had to move, and I was a little concerned
that he was going to do the same thing to me. I desperately needed
my deposit so I could move into my new place. What I expected did
happen: He told me that he was not going to give me my security
deposit and claimed that I had not left the apartment in good
enough condition. This was pretty much the same line he gave to
everyone. I knew in advance that this was a pattern of behavior with
him and that he would try to find any little thing to justify keeping
the deposit. I was greatly annoyed and angry, but this time, I felt he
had targeted the wrong person. I tried to reason with him but got
nowhere, and I was not interested in spending a lot of time in small
claims court.

I decided to go straight to my heavenly Father in prayer about
this matter. I asked the Lord to be the judge between the landlord and
me. My prayer was, "Abba Father and Lord Creator, this individual
has a record and history of not giving back tenants their security

51

deposits when they move out, and he will look for any excuse so he can hold onto their money; these people need their money so they can afford to move into another place when it's their time to leave, and You know how expensive rent is in this area. Lord, I have been approached by several people who have stated the same thing to me. So now I ask You, heavenly Father, that if I have found favor in your sight that you would please vindicate me from this wicked landlord. You have taught me, in Your Word, that I am not to take vengeance into my own hands, but I am to turn the matter over to You, and You will deal with him in Your own way and time. Amen."

I also asked the Lord God if He would answer my prayer and grant me a special request. That prayer request was this: "Since the landlord likes to keep security deposits from tenants, I ask you now, Lord, that he would not be able to rent out my unit for a year, until every penny he has erroneously taken over the years is accounted for." I specifically prayed that nobody would want to rent my previous unit until twelve months had elapsed. This would more than make up for all the money he had taken from all the tenants over the last several years. He would basically lose all the money each month for the rental of my unit for the entire year. I had remembered a scripture in the Bible where Jesus cursed a fig tree because it did not bear fruit.

So in my anger (and please excuse me, but I am only human), I asked the Lord not to let anyone rent the apartment for one year, but I also added, "Nevertheless, Thy will not mine be done." Now, that was only wishful thinking, and I never realistically thought that the King of glory would actually answer that prayer. Now you need to know that I never got back my full security deposit. However, the Lord arranged a brief encounter with me and the landlord a few years later. I just happened to run into him at a mall, and he asked me how I was doing and how things were going. I told him that everything was fine. I had completely forgotten about the security deposit he had not returned to me and about my prayer for justice.

In fact, it was not even on my mind when we met because several years had gone by.

But before the landlord left, he told me something I will never forget: "Luis, I just wanted to tell you something before I go. After you moved out, I was not able to rent out your apartment for over a year. It's the strangest thing. I painted it, put in new shelves and countertops, blinds, new carpets, and it looked really nice, and it was also located on the first floor, the unit everyone typically wants, but for some strange reason, nobody wanted to rent that particular unit in my building. It's one of the most unusual things I have ever experienced. I cannot explain it or put my finger on it. It just doesn't make any sense. Many people came to see the apartment, but nobody wanted to rent it."

After he told me this, I immediately realized that the Lord God had arranged this unplanned meeting with the landlord that day to let me know that He had answered my prayer about my security deposit and had vindicated me and the others, but I was just finding out about it now.

He went on to say, "Do you know how much money I lost by not renting out that unit for a year?"

I just smiled and whispered under my breath, "Praise God; perhaps you should not have taken all those tenants' security deposits." At this point, I realized that the Lord truly is a God of justice and that He also has a sense of humor. Although we as mere humans may forget as the years go by, He does not forget the wrongs people do to us. When we surrender our problems into His hands, He will deal with those characters and bad actors in His own time and His own way.

After the landlord left that day, I never saw him again. I am very certain that as I walked away from him, he knew deep in his heart that this all happened to him because of his prior actions toward me and the other tenants, for the Bible teaches in Galatians 6:7 that whatever you sow, you are eventually going to reap.

The Seventy-Five-Year-Old Widow

*He who has pity on the poor lends to the Lord, and He
will pay back what He has given.*

—Proverbs 19:17 (NKJV)

One afternoon, I was driving my car down the street on a quiet,
sunny day in Palo Alto, when suddenly, the Most High God spoke
to me and said, "Mary is in some trouble; she needs groceries. You
are to send her some money and be quick about it." The message
was urgent, and it startled me a little because of the intensity of the
request. I knew that this could not wait. I personally like to do things
for others toward the end of the day, when I have some extra time,
because it's more convenient for me. That's just who I am, but you
need to know that the Lord knows me better than I know myself,
so He made it a point to say, "and be quick about it."

These words challenged me to move quickly because this was
something that absolutely could not wait. It had to be done ASAP.
I knew this because I felt a heavy burden on me, and I was not at
peace. I pulled the car over, wrote a check to Mary, and went directly
to the post office and mailed it, without telling her it was on the way.
I knew Mary personally because she attended my church for several
years, so I had her contact information saved on my phone. From
the time I received the message to the time I mailed the check at the
post office, not more than thirty minutes had elapsed. I felt greatly
relieved, and a big weight was taken off my shoulders.

I thought to myself, *Man, this had to be really important;
otherwise, the message would not have been so intense, and it would
not have almost overwhelmed me.*

Three days later, Mary received the check and called me, sobbing
and crying, saying, "Thank you, thank you, thank you, for the
money. You don't know this, Luis, but exactly three days ago, I was

praying and crying out to God, because I had run out of groceries and money. I did not know what I was going to eat or how I was going to get through the month. I prayed specifically for God to touch someone to send me some money, so I could buy some food and get through the month until I received my Social Security check. You, Luis, heard God's voice and sent me the money that I desperately needed."

She thanked me half a dozen times while she cried on the phone. I told her that exactly three days ago, while I was driving my vehicle, the Lord spoke to me loudly and clearly and told me to help you. I said, "I can still remember the exact street and block I was on when I received the urgent request to help you. I immediately obeyed the voice of the Lord God, and only then was I at peace."

Oftentimes, even now, when I pass that street, I recall the spot where the Great I Am, as the God of heaven is also known, spoke to me about helping Mary. The Bible teaches that when you lend to the poor or someone in need, it is the same as lending to God, and He will pay you back in His own way and time.

Chapter 5

Developing a Christlike and Godly Character: Becoming the Word of God

Then the Lord said to Satan, "Have you considered My servant Job, that there is none like him on the earth, a blameless and upright man, one who fears God and shuns evil?"

—Job 1:8 (NKJV)

Job was a very wealthy man who had it all. He was like the Bill Gates of his day. He was particularly successful because he walked with God and was blessed with property, a business, and a great family. The devil took notice of Job and questioned God by asking Him, "If everything were taken away from Job, would he forsake You?" But the Lord knew Job's character better than anyone and knew he lived a godly life and was steadfast in his commitment to Him. Job's faith in God would not be shaken by any kind of bad news or unfortunate event that came his way; he would continue to trust Him through all the bad times and the good times.

The Lord gave the devil special permission to take from Job everything he held dear; this included his wealth, his health, his business, and his children. Despite the tragic losses he suffered, Job did not resort to sin, nor did he blame God for his misfortune. That is an example of true character. In the end, when Job's time of testing was over, God restored to him double for his losses to make up for all the trouble he went through, and God will do the same for you.

Another way we can walk in the power of the Almighty Creator is to work at developing a godly character. Having a great character is not only important to God; it's also important to your employer. As a hiring manager in the corporate world, I know that before you're hired for a job, you typically go through a screening process; this is for a good reason. They're going to ask you various questions to get a feel for the person you are, but more importantly, they are looking closely at your character. Management wants to know if you are honest, have integrity, are punctual, have a good attitude, and are a team player. They don't want to hire someone who's going to steal from them, bring everyone down, cause harm, raise red flags, or create problems for the organization. They want to know that the person they are hiring is going to be a good fit for the company.

Your character is also important to God. If He is going to bless you and answer your prayers and trust you with the responsibility to help others, then He needs you to work on your character. You need insight to manage the blessing or prayer request God is going to give you, so it does not slip right out of your hands. You will also need a certain level of maturity and discernment, so you will know how to respond in the right way when challenging circumstances arise. God is constantly testing and refining our character to see how we are going to respond to situations, so you need to get ready for that and become accustomed to it.

You need to know that God is in the character-building business; He wants to develop your character, so you'll be ready for the next level up so your life will be more fulfilling and run more smoothly. Behaving and acting inappropriately or foolishly, as you know and as God's Word warns, can cause trouble and bring big problems into your life. Acquiring a godly character is a blessing all by itself; you don't need to wait for a different sort of blessing to come.

Your character can determine your destiny and your rise and fall. Heraclitus, the Greek philosopher, said, "Character is destiny." In other words, character is king, and it is one of the things that God values the most, and therefore He desires for us to develop it in our lives. That's one reason He has given us examples of righteous people in the Bible. He wants us to learn from the experiences of others who went before us, so we can learn how to develop into the person He wants us to be.

Having a godly character is one of the keys that will open doors for you. Similarly, having a questionable character can close doors just as quickly. When you have integrity, people will get a good vibe about you and feel that you are not a shady person but someone they can trust, hang out with, and do business with. There are various individuals and countless examples in the Bible about people with outstanding character we can learn from; I have chosen just a few to highlight so you can get an idea of just how important character is to God.

> *Then the Lord said to Satan a second time: Have you considered my servant Job, that there is none like him on the Earth, a blameless and upright man, one who fears God and shuns evil?*
>
> — Job 2:3 (NKJV)

You can see the Lord God pointing out Job's character once again to Satan, the prince of darkness. This should tell you something about how important character is to God. Job's character and conduct definitely got God's attention; He wanted to show Job off to His enemy because Job was an upright and blameless individual, meaning he did not do anything wrong. Job stayed away from evil and every false way, avoiding everything he knew to be morally wrong and inappropriate. He also had a reverential and healthy fear for God. As a result, the God of heaven would eventually showcase him, speak audibly to him, answer his prayers, and bless him. But this all became possible by Job having the character that God was looking for.

Moses's character also got God's attention. The Bible records that Moses was not only rescued out of the Nile River as a baby but grew up in Pharaoh's court, where he was raised up like a prince. He learned the importance of humility through the trials and lessons he learned and experienced: "Now the man Moses was very humble, more than all men who were on the face of the earth" (Numbers 12:3 NKJV). This quality of humility was one of the main reasons that God chose him.

As I mentioned, your character is very important to God, and He wants you to make an investment in developing it. We have read the stories of how God used Moses to perform miracles and lead his people through difficulties while they marched toward the Promised Land. In fact, Moses would go on to say that he did not want to lead God's people unless the Lord's presence went with him. Joshua, his successor and another great example of godly character, would be the one who eventually led the Hebrews into the Promised Land. Moses's character and faith were principal reasons why God performed miracles through him and chose him to lead that nation. God loves humility; it's a great leadership quality.

Let's not forget the great women of the Bible, such as Hannah, Ruth, Esther, Elizabeth, and Mary. These are just a few names; there are many other women of great faith who had their own stories and were tested by God. These women also displayed godly character, overcame obstacles and disappointments, and are fitting examples of faith, courage, trust, and obedience.

One of the reasons God chose Noah to build the ark is recorded in Genesis 6:9 (NKJV): "Noah was a just man, perfect in his generations. Noah walked with God." He had the character to carry out mission impossible: The assignment God gave Noah was to save the whole human race from a worldwide flood. Having a righteous and honorable character is very important to the Creator, and it will help you in all areas of your life, both personally and professionally. Developing these traits is also important for promotion and advancement. Holiness and godly living is the Lord's standard, and it will bring you joy, happiness, and fulfillment to your life.

The Bible also talks about developing what's called the fruit of the spirit. These character traits and qualities are spelled out in Galatians 5:22–23 (NKJV): "But the fruit of the Spirit is love, joy, peace, longsuffering, kindness, goodness, faithfulness, gentleness, self-control. Against such there is no law." These are qualities He would also like us to develop.

The opposite of righteousness is sin: doing what you know is morally wrong and unethical. Although doing what is wrong, whatever it may be, might be briefly pleasurable, it can set you back years and will eventually bring sorrow and suffering into your life. One law that applies universally is the principle of sowing and reaping: Whatever you plant or do in your life, you eventually will reap, and it will come back to you. It's also known as karma. What you do is eventually going to find you; sinful behavior will eventually catch up with you. People may not realize that the payback typically arrives in another season. Don't cut corners; listen to the Lord, and stay away from all things that you know in your heart and mind are morally wrong and inappropriate (or, as God says, sinful in nature). The answers to your prayers really depend on adhering to this principle.

One of the main purposes for reading the Bible is to help you develop a Christlike character; it is one of the principal goals. The character of Jesus, the Son of God and our Savior, is the greatest example there is. His character is perfect in every way. He showed us how to walk and live our lives with integrity, righteousness, and holiness. There is much we can learn from His teachings and His conduct, and I encourage you to read and study Christ's life which can be found in the gospels of Matthew, Mark, Luke, and John so you can learn about this person whose character was flawless. Holiness is God's standard: "Be holy, for I am holy" (1 Peter 1:16 NKJV). Learning to love people, being patient and understanding, performing random acts of kindness, and forgiving others is God's preferred way of conducting ourselves. Once you develop your character, the Lord can begin to honor you and answer your prayers. He will also use you, like some of these people in the Bible, to make a difference in the world around you. He desires to use a clean and pure vessel to reach those in need, but He can use anyone at any time, if He chooses. However, He does prefer to use a person of integrity and good character to deliver a message or render assistance. The Lord has used me many times to make an impact in the community where I live, and it's a beautiful feeling knowing I am being used by the Almighty Creator to make a difference in the lives of people around me. It all begins with prayer, devotion, and developing a godly character. God does not want us to just read His Word; He also wants us to apply His Word in our lives. The Lord ultimately desires that we live and become like His Word, and we can do that by emulating our Savior, Jesus Christ. Please keep in mind that Christ does have a special plan for your life; the plan will be revealed to you as you draw near to Him and receive His free gift of salvation.

> *For God so loved the world that He gave His only begotten Son, that whoever believes in Him should not perish but have everlasting life.*

> — John 3:16 (NKJV)

Here is a story you might find amusing: One morning, as I was praying about my character, I asked the Lord if He would use me that week to be eyes for the blind and feet for the lame. This request was as a result of a scripture I had read during my daily devotion. I clearly remember quoting the prayer that morning. That afternoon on my lunch break, I decided to leave the office to eat. I was at the corner of a busy intersection, waiting for the light to change. As the light turned green, I began to walk; just then, someone with dark sunglasses suddenly and forcibly grabbed my arm as I was about to cross the street. This person did not ask for my permission at all; he just grabbed my arm firmly, like he knew me, and told me, "I need you to take me to the other end of the street," as though I was his personal caretaker.

I was a little shocked and surprised at his aggressive maneuver because I did not know him; I had not even noticed him at the corner. I took him across the street anyway because I realized that he was blind and could not see; I noticed he had difficulty walking too. As I got halfway through this long, wide street in the heart of the San Francisco financial district, I realized that God was using me to be eyes for the blind and feet for the lame. My prayer had been answered in an unexpected way. Please be careful what you pray for because the God of all the earth just might take you up on it. As I mentioned previously, it's a wonderful privilege knowing you are being used by Almighty God to fulfill His purpose and help someone in need.

> *Believe me Sir, never a night goes by, be I ever so tired, but I read the Word of God before I go to bed.*

> —General Douglas MacArthur

The Atheist

> *For the message of the cross is foolishness to those who are perishing, but to us who are being saved it is the power of God.*

> —1 Corinthians 1:18 (NKJV)

I had received a full scholarship to a university in San Francisco, and I was working toward a bachelor's degree in business management. One of the classes I was required to take was philosophy. My instructor was one of the most well-read professors I have ever encountered. I was in awe of his intelligence and admired his ability to teach. Up to that point, I had never seen an instructor directly quote so many authors of books in a single class setting. He had read all these books and quoted these authors and books every ten minutes. By the time each class session had ended, he had quoted and named about a dozen or more authors, and then he was able to tie up the loose ends and bring all the information together to make his point. This was truly impressive. I marveled at his brilliance, teaching style, and intellectual ability. I really enjoyed being in his class; not only was I learning a great deal, but I developed a great respect for him.

One day, he mentioned that we were required to give a speech and submit a paper on any philosophy topic we chose. Well naturally, since I had the encounter with the Creator, I wanted to share with the class my incredible experience and share with my classmates what I believe to be the truth about my philosophy for living. On the day when I was to deliver my speech, I went into the bathroom and prayed silently for a few minutes. I went into the classroom and began my speech by explaining that what I was about to say was my personal belief only, and that I was not trying to indoctrinate, persuade, or convince anyone to follow me or convert them in any way. I wanted them to understand that these ideas were only what I believed and what I based my philosophy for living on.

The students nodded their heads in approval, so I felt good about sharing my thoughts and beliefs freely. I shared with them the fantastic story that I had experienced about my encounter with the Creator; several students found this intriguing, and after class, some of them even asked me more about it. I also talked about the Bible and how I believe it is the Creator's manual for living here on earth. I mentioned that a lot of the violence and crime we experience is due to people not following the basic instructions and commandments of the Bible; for example, don't steal, kill, murder, or commit adultery.

Not one student complained or said anything derogatory to me after the class. In fact, they applauded and thanked me and said that my speech was pretty good. To my surprise, everyone liked the speech, except my professor. What I did not realize is that two opposing schools of thought regarding the existence of the Creator were about to clash. On one side was a PhD philosophy teacher who was very well-read, highly educated, and a committed atheist. On the other side was a college kid, with no degree, but who had a real-life physical encounter with the Almighty God and Creator. We were headed for a direct collision.

My professor was livid. He angrily complained to the whole class that my presentation was not philosophy and claimed that there was no God. I thought, *Wow, I did not see that coming.* He gave me a dirty look, or what I should really call a look of disapproval; he was very disappointed in me. He then used the rest of the class time to destroy my position and tear down any argument supporting the existence of God, and he gave me a D- for my presentation and my paper. He went on this same rampage for the next several months. Naturally, I found his approach unnerving and very uncomfortable because he was attempting to dismantle what I had presented, in addition to negating any notion of God's existence.

This scenario would happen at every class session for the next couple of months. I was not sure why he was so angry with God; perhaps something tragic happened to him in his life. I was in serious trouble because I was on a scholarship and would lose it if my grades slipped. It did not help that this instructor was consistently giving me angry looks, like he did not appreciate me or even want me in his class.

I kept quiet the whole time and decided the best approach was to not retaliate but instead activate my faith, so I went right to work on the problem. I began to pray to the Lord and let Him know that I was in serious trouble. "Lord God Almighty," I prayed, "I put my neck out to tell the world about You and our encounter and Your greatness, and now my professor, this walking Encyclopedia Britannica, not to mention the smartest professor I have ever had, has turned on me, and now I believe he wants to fail me. Please help me and show me what to do." I was prompted to pray specifically for this professor with the following words: "Lord Creator, I pray that you will illuminate his understanding so that he will begin to see You in all the philosophies and books that he has ever read. I also pray that You will help him connect the dots and solve the missing pieces of the puzzle, so he can begin to see You in all the knowledge and teachings he has acquired."

I prayed nonstop for my instructor, the atheist, so he could somehow have a real-life experience with God. I prayed especially that I wouldn't fail the class because of my speech. It was a long semester for me, but I just kept praying, believing and trusting God; however, nothing seemed to happen or change whatsoever.

The fool has said in his heart, "There is no God."

— Psalm 14:1 (NKJV)

Then three weeks before the end of the semester and the final class meeting, something spectacular happened. The professor asked me to come to his office. I thought, *Oh boy, this is it; he is definitely going to fail me now.* Up to that point, I had done all right on the other exams but was not really sure where I stood with my final grade. But then, to my great surprise, he said, "Luis, I want to apologize to you for the way I have acted toward you and by saying there is no God. You see, I have held atheistic views all my life, but the other day, something or someone spoke to me, and now I have come to realize that I was wrong and now I see clearly that there is a God."

I was speechless, flabbergasted. I'm not exactly sure what the Lord God said to him or what he experienced, because he never told me, but whatever it was, it made him realize that I was telling the truth and that there definitely is a higher power. As I sat in his office listening to him, I could see in his eyes, demeanor, and speech that he was a changed man and that something truly extraordinary had happened to him. He went on to say that what also helped him to understand that there is a God was the concept of stewardship. This concept is also found in the Bible. In the Bible, stewardship means we have a responsibility and obligation to take care of and manage the things God has given us; we are accountable to Him for what we do with everything we have because it all comes from Him anyway, so we must respect that which He has entrusted to us and not be wasteful or mismanage things.

It turned out to be the missing link for him, and once he understood how stewardship has a universal application, it helped him connect the dots on the various teachings and philosophies. It all made sense to him now, he stated. My prayer for him was answered.

Now this story gets even better, because after that office visit, to my surprise, he went in front of the whole class and said, "I just want everyone to know that I was wrong and that I now see that there is God." He then discussed at great length, and in much detail, the concept of stewardship and how it relates to various philosophies. I ended up passing the class without a problem and thanked God for His divine intervention and deliverance. I then told the Lord, "Boy, that was really close, but You were right on time."

The Turkey with a Testimony

> *And we know that all things work together for good to those who love God, to those who are the called according to His purpose.*
>
> —Romans 8:28 (NKJV)

We arranged a holiday party for a Bible study group at a firm I use to work for; it was a potluck luncheon scheduled for the week of Thanksgiving. Everyone agreed to bring something for the potluck. Since I was one of the leaders of the Bible study group, I agreed to bring the turkey. The week before the potluck, I looked for a place that could sell us a large enough turkey for all of us. I found a place not too far from my firm and ordered the turkey for the appointed day. When I purchased the turkey, I was told by the clerk that it would be hot and ready to serve; however, when I went to pick it up, it had mistakenly been left in a refrigerator all night. Apparently, there was some miscommunication with the deli worker at the store. I'm not sure if he was a new employee or just got my order wrong. But whatever the reason, I had a cold turkey on my hands and about thirty guests arriving shortly. I was in a terrible jam.

I had just left the conference room where we would be celebrating the luncheon, and the room was full of side dishes and desserts. Everything you could imagine for a Thanksgiving dinner was ready, except for the star of the show: the turkey None of the guests had a clue about the mistake that had happened; no one suspected that I was on the way back with a cold turkey. I was in trouble and didn't know what to do about the situation.

I thought to myself, *I really made a mess of this, and everyone will be arriving within the hour. What do I do now?*

There was no option I could think of, except perhaps to microwave the turkey; however, I knew that it would never fit inside a microwave, so I decided to pray, "Heavenly Father and Lord God Almighty, I need a miracle, and I need it within an hour. Please show me what to do."

I explained to the Lord what happened at the deli. Now the Lord already knows everything, and especially how my turkey order got botched, but I wanted to tell Him anyway, to get it off my chest. I prayed about this situation the whole ride back to the office; however, I did not hear a single word back from Him. I got no response at all.

So I just kept my cool, as I normally do in these situations, and tried not to panic but kept trusting God.

I said to myself, *God will show up and make a way somehow.* I parked my vehicle, and as I was getting ready to get out of the car, still feeling disappointed in myself and honestly a little worried, the Lord suddenly spoke to me and said these words: "Bring the turkey to your Latino brothers, and they will know what to do, for I have instructed them what to do." Now I heard those words crystal clear and knew it was the Lord speaking to me, the same way He always does, and knew that He was showing me how He was going to resolve this problem. I also knew immediately which Latino brothers He was referring to, because there was a small group of professional chefs and cooks who worked in the kitchen and prepared the meals for the entire firm. The Lord was going to get me out of the mess I got myself into. But honestly, I still had a few lingering doubts. I thought to myself, *What if there is a long line of people waiting to have lunch, or a supervisor on duty that says, "No, we can't do that for you; we just don't have the time, space, or capacity to help you today."*

Besides all of this, I did not know any of the cooks or chefs personally, so all these questions raced wildly through my mind as I approached the company's cafeteria. I would have to put all those doubts aside for a moment and trust the Lord and His words, as I always do in these situations. Those words "your Latino brothers" kept replaying in my mind because I had never heard someone say that to me ever in my life. God was reminding me that they are my brothers and that I come from this Latino lineage. Although I was born in the United States and spoke only a little Spanish, I was being reminded that they were my brothers and were there to help me.

I would like to point out something to you about the Lord when He speaks to you. Notice how the Lord said to me, "They will know what to do, for I have instructed them what to do." You see, God did not give me the instructions, detailed plans, or blueprints on how the cooks were going to fix this. It would be, as it always is, a walk of faith. Faith and trust please God. I was simply told to bring the turkey to them and then trust God to work it out.

As I approached the kitchen, the first chef I saw happened to be Latino; it was someone I didn't even know. I said in Spanish, "*Hola, hermano*" (Hello, brother). I thought, *Well, why not? They are my brothers, right?* I then started to explain the situation to him. As I began telling the chef the problem, he interrupted me after a couple of seconds and said he already knew what to do. I just looked at him rather curiously and said to myself, *Okay, praise God; I guess he got the memo.* However, I did get a chance to tell him before I left that I had thirty guests waiting and asked if he could please get something ready for them. He told me to return in forty minutes. This interaction with the chef happened so fast that I knew the Lord was in control of the situation and this miracle was under way. I was experiencing it in real time.

When I returned forty-five minutes later, to my surprise, the chef had cut thirty hot turkey slices and had arranged them beautifully on a large platter. The plate was adorned like something right out of a five-star restaurant. The kitchen also gave me gravy, stuffing, and cranberry sauce, which I had not even asked for. Apparently, they just happened to be cooking turkey that week for the employees of the firm. He told me to come back and pick up the rest of the turkey as soon as I had an opportunity.

I arrived at the conference room where the potluck was taking place, right on time and on schedule; everyone was there. I did not tell anybody about what had happened with the turkey until everyone was done eating and full. About an hour later, once everyone had eaten and was about to leave, I then told everyone that this turkey had a testimony of its own. I then proceeded to tell them the story. They all laughed and said it was one of the best turkeys they had ever eaten and one of the best Thanksgiving stories they had heard; they thanked the Lord for His divine intervention.

But this story does not end there; I had also asked the Lord to bless that turkey so there would be plenty of leftovers to feed the multitudes in various other practice groups. The turkey that was blessed by God ended up feeding lots of other people. I just said that prayer like I normally do, not expecting anything out of the ordinary. What ended up happening next completely surprised me, and I would have to say it was certainly supernatural and miraculous. The turkey that was left over from the Bible study group and that was only supposed to feed a couple dozen guests somehow ended up feeding about a hundred people.

I don't know how it was possible; the math certainly does not add up or even make any sense to me. Additionally, I did not see the turkey multiplying before my eyes in any visible way, but somehow, it was not entirely consumed until everyone had eaten. That delicious turkey was completely gone at the end of the day. It was truly fantastic. I just stood there, amazed, and wondered how any of this was possible; I have never seen or experienced anything like this before. This turkey definitely had a testimony.

Chapter 6

The Power of Praise and Worship: Unlocking the Gates of Heaven

But you are a chosen generation, a royal priesthood, a holy nation, His own special people, that you may proclaim the praises of Him who called you out of darkness and into His marvelous light; who once were not a people but are now the people of God, who had not obtained mercy but now have obtained mercy.

—1 Peter 2:9-10 (NKJV)

The Lord said to Abram, "Get out of your country and away from your family and your father's house and go to a land that I will show you." So Abram, whose name would later be changed to Abraham (a father of nations), went out, not knowing where he was going. He prayed and asked God, "Where do you want me to go?" The Lord basically told him, "Start walking. I'll let you know when you get there."

Abraham is a great example of obedience, faith, and trust. He praised God through his earthly trials such as being willing to offer his son as a sacrifice to the Lord in an act of trust and worshipped

God through his honorable lifestyle on his journey to the Promised Land. Abraham believed in the Lord, and it was accounted to him as righteousness. Another way we can begin to walk in the power of the Almighty Creator is through actively participating each week in praise and worship. Books can be written on this subject alone, but I would just like briefly illustrate in this chapter why this is important to the Lord.

Now Paul and Silas, the servants of God, had been ministering the Lord's word in a certain province, and on their way to a place of prayer, found themselves arrested and charged for casting out a spirit of divination from a slave girl who had been following and harassing them. As a result of the spirit leaving the slave girl, who just happened to be a fortune teller, she was now unable to make any more money for her master from her occupation as a fortune teller. So her master pressed charges against Paul and Silas, according to the laws at the time. Paul and Silas were accused of causing trouble and of being Jews, and teaching customs which the master said were not lawful. They were severely beaten, flogged and whipped, and were cast into a prison, and their hands and feet were bound with chains and shackles.

However, at midnight Paul and Silas began to praise God by singing songs and hymns and worshipped God with prayer. Suddenly, the Lord caused a great earthquake which shook the foundations of the prison, causing all of the prison doors to open wide, and all the shackles or chains on their hands and feet broke free and were loosed. The jailer who guarded them woke up in a panic, very afraid, and thought that they had escaped. The guard was about to take his own life with his sword, but right before he did so, Paul told him not to end his life because they were still in their jail cell and had not fled. The jailer, seeing the power of God and the miracle which had just happened, was overcome with awe and emotion and, trembling, asked Paul what he must do to be saved. Paul would go on to tell him more about God's love and Christ's saving power. The following morning the Lord also had the local magistrate release them and set them free. However, Paul was not satisfied and went on to challenge the reason he was placed in the prison in the first place.

Paul and Silas's simple act of praise and worshipping the Lord not only unlocked the gates of heaven, releasing God's power to help them, but also directly caused the unlocking of the prison doors and the chains that bound them. The way God helped them and set them free from their circumstance through an act of praise and worship, is the way he will help you and deliver you out of any situation you may find yourself stuck in. You can read more about this in the sixteenth chapter of the book of Acts.

The God of heaven wants to be praised, acknowledged, and thanked for each day we are given. He wants to be honored for all He has done for you in your life and in the lives of others, whether you're consciously aware of it or not. Thank Him with your mouth each day in prayer and worship Him every day with your living and giving. He desires a life that is surrendered to Him and His will. He wants us to be His special and distinctive people, to declare His praise among all nations. We are His special treasure. We are the light of the world, a city on a hill for all to see, which cannot be hid. When we worship Him in spirit and in truth, we shine as lights in a dark, perverse, and corrupt world.

We are also the salt of the earth. In other words, we give flavor to the world and make it a more interesting and pleasant place. When we tell others about the wonderful things He has done for us and through us, we are praising and worshipping Him. This gives hope to others who are struggling, asleep, or walking along the wrong path. God the Father wants us to be a doer of His Word, not just a talker or hearer of the Word. We must not only honor God with our lips and mouths but honor Him with our hearts and actions, as well. If you say you love God and desire to know Him, but then turn a blind eye to someone in need the Lord sent your way, then it's not the kind of love, compassion, or response He wants from you.

You cannot help the entire world, and the Lord does not expect you to; however, you can do your small part to help the ones in your arena of influence and the ones He sends directly to you. Your actions speak much louder than your words, and they tell the true story of who you really are. God knows everything you do in private and what you do publicly. You can say all you want that you are a godly person, but if your actions don't show it or line up with God's Word, then you are only fooling yourself.

There is a big difference between being good and being godly. Being godly is going the extra mile to please God. It's responding in a Christlike manner with love, forgiveness, understanding, patience, gentleness, and kindness: these are God-like qualities. We can worship God daily by how we live and by how we give our time and resources to others in need.

Faith without works is dead.

— James 2:26 (NKJV)

One thing that pleases God the most is when you are going through a trial, a difficult time, or an unusual tough circumstance, and you still praise and worship Him like nothing has happened in your life at all. You are completely trusting Him and not worrying about a thing because you have read His Word, the Bible, and you know the end of every matter: It's you being victorious with God at your side. Keep in mind that one person walking with God is always a majority; you really can't lose when you're walking in His power. When you do that, things will always turn out well for you, one way or another.

This kind of faith confuses the demons the enemy sends your way to get you off course; it drives them absolutely nuts. When you're going through traumatic times or facing something particularly challenging, just keep smiling and don't complain. Adopt a good attitude and thank God for seeing you through it all, without worry or fear. Enjoy your day, no matter what the problem is. This type of faith, praise, and worship will unlock the gates of heaven for you and will give the devil a heart attack and every demon assigned to you a nervous breakdown. They won't stand a chance against you because of your trust in God, and they will not know what to do about you except leave you alone for a while.

Those demons will leave, shaking their heads in confusion, and will tell their big boss, "We did everything we could to discourage him, but it's just not working, so let's find someone else to mess with. We are wasting too much time here." The Bible says to resist the devil, and he will flee from you (James 4:7). You can resist that crafty serpent by behaving righteously, having a godly character, and praising and worshipping God each day. Now if there is a God, and I know there is because I have met Him personally, then you better believe there are demons, ghosts, and unclean spirits running amuck, trying to make your life miserable. That's their job, so don't panic, but you do need to be aware of it.

These entities show up in your life when you open the door through sinful behavior or by hanging out with people who have been compromised. When you are doing bad things—and you know what those things are—you are opening the front door for demons to come into your life and influence you. I have a news flash for you: These turkeys are not your pals. They are destructive in nature and are there to separate you from God, take you out of God's purpose for your life, and influence you through poor decision making, immoral choices, and clouded thinking, so you end up losing everything God has given you. One of their jobs is to steal, kill, and destroy just about everything you love; for instance, a good job, a beautiful marriage, a family, a nice house, a best friend, children, and so on. Sin in your life will cause you to lose these important things.

That's why it's important to walk with God and continually praise and worship Him; this will drive those unclean spirits far away from you, your job, and your home. When you feel like everything is going wrong in your day, it could be that those unclean spirits are hanging around you, making a mess of things and trying to discourage and frustrate you; however, you cannot see them because they are in the spiritual realm. Just rebuke them in the name of Jesus, and they will leave you alone. Close the doors to sin in your life, whether it is drug abuse, pornography, theft, adultery, alcoholism, violence, unclean thoughts, or sexual immorality. These demonic entities are counting on you to let them in by succumbing to sinful pleasures instead of making godly sacrifices and having a healthy lifestyle. They want you to succumb to selfish and evil desires in order to have access to you so they can then work at taking everything away from you, but when you praise and worship the God of heaven on a daily basis, those pathetic and hideous creatures don't have a chance. They'll have no choice but to flee from you. Don't let these unclean spirits ruin your life by engaging in sinful self-indulgence due to a lack of discipline. Be honorable and righteous, and work on your character every day; say no to sin and yes to God. Your bright future depends on it. That's the kind of faith and trust the Lord wants you to have.

Over the years, I have learned to enjoy an ice cream cone in the middle of the storms of life. Being able to praise and worship God in the middle of trial and uncertainty is what pleases Him because it shows that we trust Him. I don't worry too much anymore about anything. I just take action and attack the problem and work at resolving it to the best of my ability. People who know me have never seen me freak out about anything. I just tell them it's because I walk with God. His power is with me, and I know through past experience that it's all going to turn out well in the end, so there really is no need to waste my time worrying.

I've been down that road several times, and it always ends well, and rest assured it will for you too. Just act responsibly, and He will help you get through every challenge, no matter what it is; just ask for His help. You see, I already know that He has my back, for the Bible says He is your rear guard, and everything is going to turn out all right. When you praise Him and worship Him regularly, you will worry less because you know deep down inside, He is with you and will see you through it all, just as He has always done. If you look back at your life at all the things you've been through, you should be able to see evidence that He has always made a way for you when there seemed to be no way. He has carried you all this way and is not about to quit on you now because He is your heavenly Father and loves you more than you can ever imagine.

Not forsaking the assembling of ourselves together, as is the manner of some, but exhorting one another, and so much the more as you see the Day approaching.

— Hebrews 10:25 (NKJV)

Going to church or a house of worship is very important for your spiritual growth and development; it's a basic form of worship. It's in God's house that we get a chance to praise Him in song and dance and worship Him with our hands raised heavenward with other believers. In His house, we also get a chance to hear the reading of His Word from an ordained minister, priest, or pastor; this will encourage you, shed light on various topics, and prepare you for living with moral excellence in this challenging world.

Gathering with other like-minded individuals is also how we get an opportunity to encourage each other, by learning about the miraculous things God is doing in the lives of others. It's also a great place to meet people, make friends, and most importantly, have a second family. If you are feeling lonely and have few friends, I encourage you to get into a house of worship in your community; you will find some of the most loving and wonderful people you have ever known. God's house is also a place where we have an opportunity to give financially to support the work of that ministry. I encourage you to give an offering so that the Lord will give it back to you in ways money cannot buy.

When the God of heaven sees you attending a house of worship,

He will bless you with a very good week, season, and year. I have personally noticed the difference when I attend a weekly service and when I don't. My work week runs a lot smoother because His Holy Spirit of wisdom is there to guide me as I make decisions and choices, and His blessing goes with me wherever I go. I feel loved, safe, and happy. It's a beautiful feeling, and it's supernatural. Have you ever wondered why church people smile a lot and look so happy all the time? It's because God's power is on them; they know it and can feel it, and it shows.

> *That book, the Bible, is the Rock on which our Republic rests.*
>
> —Andrew Jackson

A Breakfast Story

> *The Lord does not let the righteous go hungry, but He thwarts the craving of the wicked.*
>
> — Proverbs 10:3 (NIV)

One morning, I was sitting in my car at a McDonald's parking lot, waiting for a coworker to arrive so I could start my day, when suddenly, the Lord, who is also known as Jehovah Jireh (the God who provides), spoke to me and said, "The man who is standing in front of you is hungry, and you are to buy him breakfast."

This statement was loud and crystal clear; it was definitely a command, not a request, and I knew I had to do it.

I just whispered, "All right, I will do it."

Whenever the Creator speaks to you, you experience a sense of urgency from His message, and you feel compelled to do it, but in a cheerful and good way. You can refuse the command if you want, but if you do, don't expect Him to be using you to help others anytime soon. You may need to get your heart and mind right with Him first, as the Bible stipulates. Also, His message is typically short and to the point. In other words, He does not waste words; He gets to the heart of the matter quickly.

As He said these words to me, I began looking for this individual. I immediately noticed a thin man about fifty yards from my car. However, he was not looking at me at all and did not even seem to notice me; all I could see was the back of his head. I then noticed him walking away from where I was parked.

I thought to myself, *Okay, I am off the hook; he is leaving the area, so it looks like I won't need to buy him breakfast after all, unless he is redirected to me by God,* but then suddenly, he changed course, turned around, and walked directly to my vehicle. He knocked on my window, so I lowered it and asked how I could help him (but I already knew the answer before I even asked).

He said, "Can you please buy me some breakfast?"

I said, to the annoyance of my coworker, "Sure, what would you like?"

He smiled and said, "A number 3 breakfast with a coffee."

I said, "Okay, I will be right back; wait here."

It only took a few minutes to get his breakfast, and I only spent about seven dollars, which I could easily afford. I was in and out quickly. I would like to note that God miraculously moved everyone out of the way, so I could complete this mission in no time and not interrupt my day.

My coworker was furious and mumbled under her breath, "Don't buy him anything. He looks healthy enough to work. He should get a job."

When I returned a few minutes later and brought him his breakfast, he said, "Thank you," and began to walk away.

But before he left, I said, "Excuse me?"

He said, "Yes?"

Then I said, "What made you come to my vehicle?"

He said, "God told me that the man in this car [my car] would be buying me breakfast today."

My coworker was utterly stunned, and her mouth literally dropped open. I then told her that when the Lord asks you to help someone in need, it's a noble thing to show mercy and compassion, lest you find yourself in a similar position. In other words, be the vessel that He is going to use to make a difference in someone's life and in the world.

I would like to point out two things to you: First, when the Creator speaks to you about helping someone in need, He usually speaks to you and to the other person also, and it's often at the exact same time. This is one way to confirm it's Him talking to you: You both get the message. The second thing is, when this happens, He will typically bring that person directly to you, so you don't have to go searching for them. The Lord will make it very easy for you to show a random act of kindness; you just need to decide whether you are going to respond in the right way, with love and compassion, or harden your heart like a stone.

The Millionaire

> *His Divine power has given us everything we need for a Godly life through our knowledge of Him who called us by His own glory and goodness.*

> —2 Peter 1:3 (NIV)

One Saturday morning, I got up early and went to pray at a park in my neighborhood. It was around seven o'clock, and it was cold out. I didn't care about the weather because I was upset by my best friend's personality change after he had become a millionaire through a new business venture, an importing/exporting mining operation business based out of Africa. He had shown me his ATM bank receipt at one point, just to show off, and it read that he had $10 million in his account. At twenty-three years old, he had purchased a mansion and several luxury vehicles, new fancy clothes, and expensive jewelry, and it did not help that a helicopter would pick him up sometimes just to take him to lunch. Not bad for a young man his age, and I must say it was impressive.

What bothered me was not just the money he acquired but his new attitude toward God and my relationship with the Lord. At the time, all I could afford to rent was a room in a house, and I was a little older than him, so you can imagine how all this made me feel. We had met at the university, when he was a devout Christian. At that time, he was in a good relationship with the Lord and was able to quote many scriptures at will, but once he got all the money, he had walked away from God and now had no interest in serving the Lord any longer. He would playfully mock me at times for going to church and for praying.

I, on the other hand, had a full-time job at a law office and was attending Sunday services each week and praying and reading the Bible daily to strengthen my relationship with God. I also devoted a couple of hours every Saturday to our church ministry, helping feed the homeless in my community. I did this for several years, but my best friend would mock me for it, saying it was a waste of my time. Honestly, I was a little jealous of his financial situation, because he was very successful and would show off all his fancy cars, which included Mercedes, Porsches, and BMWs that were all valued well over a $100,000 each. He flaunted his newfound wealth and pretty girls around me regularly and then had the audacity to tell me there was no God.

I thought to myself, *The pharaoh of the Egyptian empire said the same thing to Moses, just before his army was destroyed.* My friend's behavior was a real test for me: Would I get angry and walk away from God because I was not as successful as my best friend, or would I remain faithful and committed to Him, no matter what? I asked the Lord that Saturday morning, "Why do you allow my best friend to prosper when he refuses to honor and even acknowledge You? Here I am, doing my best to walk with You and include You in my daily devotion, and I am just getting by, living paycheck to paycheck."

I prayed this way for about an hour, complaining to the Lord about why I was not financially successful. I was discouraged, angry, and confused. Suddenly, the Lord spoke to me by asking one question. He asked, "Am I not better to you than all the wealth of this world?"

Wow. I didn't know what to say or how to answer that question. How could I argue with such a profound statement? I was speechless. And then He immediately gave me another revelation: He, the Lord God Almighty, is my healer when I get sick. He is the one who encourages me when I am feeling down. He is the one who provides companionship for me when I am lonely, and He is the one who will provide a mate for me when the time is right. He is the one who promotes me at my place of employment. He is the one who lifts me up when I am brought down. He is the one who directs my steps and leads my life in a godly manner. This was all revealed to me in a few seconds when He spoke to me.

It was also revealed to me that if my best friend were to become critically ill someday, all his wealth would not be able to save him. The revelation ended with these words: "I Am everything you will ever need." The Great I Am, as God is also known, fixed my attitude problem and my complaining by just asking me one simple question. After He asked me this question, it put things in perspective for me, and I felt a lot better. I would also like to mention that one day the Lord touched my best friend's heart to write me a check in order to pay off my student loans. It was an act of generosity which I really appreciated.

From that day forward, I never complained or questioned the Lord again about my best friend or his wealth, but instead, I put my trust in the Lord, who reminded me that He truly is all I will ever need in this life, and He will provide for me all that is necessary for my happiness and well-being. I just needed to trust Him and learn to walk with him.

By the way, several years later, my best friend ended up losing his millions, his mansion, his luxury cars, and the pretty girls too by mismanaging his wealth. You see, he may have gotten the money through hard work and some smart business decisions early on, but in my opinion, he did not have the godly wisdom and discipline to manage the wealth and grow his business successfully.

This story ends with me, a decade later, loaning him money on numerous occasions so that he could just get by. I knew, from God's revelation, that at some point in my future, the tables would turn, and we would switch roles financially; I ended up in a greater financial position, helping him, but with my godly character intact.

Chapter 7

The Reconciliation of a Father and Son: A Tale of Two Fathers

When my father and my mother forsake me, then the Lord will take care of me.

—Psalm 27:10 (NKJV)

It had been over twenty years since I had last spoken to my father. The last time I had seen him, I was a fifteen-year-old kid, and I was glad to get away from that situation. Life with him had been a nightmare that seemed to have no end. My father had been an alcoholic in his younger days; he had a violent temper, had some mental health issues, and could be very abusive. It also did not help that my mother and father had married very young. She was only fourteen years old, and he was around twenty. This is not permissible in the United States, however; this was common at the time in many Central American countries. They both only had a fourth grade level education, so I am certain this impacted their marriage.

My mother left him when I was only two, because she could not endure his verbal and physical abuse; he constantly made threats against her. He was unstable and dangerous and had been arrested several times for assaulting her. She eventually filed a restraining order with the police and then left, taking me and Michael, my brother, and Jacqueline and Xiomara, my sisters, with her. The threat of arrest and a new job opportunity prompted my father to move to New Jersey, New York, and then Chicago.

As a single mom, my mother raised four children by herself while living on welfare, and as you can imagine, we did not live in the best neighborhood. It was a rough start and a tough place to grow up. My father had once proudly boasted to me that he was the leader of a gang in the San Francisco Mission District in the early 1960s; he told me how much he loved violence and enjoyed fighting with other rival gangs. This helped explain why he was abusive toward his family.

The first time I saw my father was at the airport in Chicago. I was about seven years old; I was a little afraid of him and did not really trust him. I felt instinctively that he was not very loving or nurturing; there was something about him that was not right, and I felt that he was not trustworthy. I had not seen him since I was very young and had no recollection of him until I met him at O'Hare International Airport. My mother had sent me and Michael to stay with him for the summer because he had been asking about us. But when it came time to send us back to my mother in California, he deliberately moved away, changed addresses, disconnected the telephone, and told us stories that our mother had abandoned us.

This happened in the early 1970s, and I did not see or hear from my mother for the next year and a half. I just remember feeling scared and missing my mother all the time; I would stare out the window and wonder when she was going to come and pick us up. My father was often depressed and not very nice to us; he could be mean-spirited at times and was constantly on the move.

The first time I can remember when he mistreated me occurred one night when I wasn't feeling well. I tried to wake him up to let him know I needed to throw up. But he would not wake up because he was in a deep sleep and did not hear me calling to him. As it so happened, Michael and I and my father all slept on the same bed in a basement garage because he did not have a lot of money. I was running a high fever and threw up on the bed where we slept. My father finally woke up; he got very angry and began to scream and shout at me. He then grabbed me by the hair on the back of my head and repeatedly smashed my face directly into my own vomit on the bed.

When he was done doing this to me, I had my own vomit dripping from my face, my mouth, and my clothes, and it was all over my hair. He then forced me to go clean myself up in the bathroom. I was crying for my mother the whole time, but there would be no mother around to hear my plea for help. I could not figure out why this man was always so angry and such a miserable wretch of a person (I later found out that he suffered from some mental health issues).

He rarely talked to me and often told me that I wasn't really his child, which hurt my feelings and wasn't true, of course. I can honestly say that I don't have any memories of him ever giving me a hug or saying that he loved me. I am not sure why he even wanted us there.

I recall another time he got very angry at me; I don't even remember why, because I was just a little boy of seven or eight years old, but nevertheless, he got on top of me and sat on me and pinned me down, so I could not move my arms. He began to strike me, hitting and slapping my face repeatedly. My nose began to bleed, and almost instantly, my whole face was full of blood, and so were his hands. When he saw how bad it was, he got off me. He was breathing very heavily and looked really scared, like he just almost killed me; maybe that's why he jumped off me. He then screamed, "My God, what have I done?" and then carried me to the bathroom in a panic to clean and wash me up.

After this event, he backed off me and was nice to me for the next couple of weeks. I guess he was afraid or worried that I was going to report him to somebody or tell my mother whenever I saw her. I could only imagine what things he had done to my mother, and I did not blame her for leaving him.

I often wondered where she was, what she was doing, and when she was going to pick us up. One day, the doorbell rang, and much to my surprise, it was my mother at the door. It had been almost two years since I had seen her. Michael and I were at home alone in a new place we had moved to. My father was at work and was not aware of my mother's visit. Somehow, she found our address and waited for my father to leave to go work. She stealthily approached the house and pleaded with us to let her in. We opened the door for her, and she gave us both hugs and then told us to get our things because we were leaving. I was so happy to see her and could not believe she was really there; it seemed like a dream. The next thing I knew, we were all on an airplane, heading back to California. My father did not know where we were until that night, when my mother called to let him know she took us back with her to California.

It was a bold move on her part, and you've got to give my mother credit because it took guts for her to come to Chicago all alone to get her kids and take them back home without anyone finding out. It was also dangerous; she was afraid of him because of the beatings he gave her, but she managed to pull it off. I told my mother everything that had happened, including the abuse, but she did not want to believe me; I guess it was too much for her to take.

We stayed in California for a few years. I was glad to be away from the nightmare of living with this menacing father figure. Then when I was about ten years old, my father asked about us again, according to my mother. Figuring he got the message the first time, and since we were a little older, she decided it was okay to send Michael, me, and Jacqueline back again to see him for a short while. I protested, but there was nothing I could do: I was heading back to that place of torment.

That would end up being the darkest years of my life, but it also was the beginning of God's divine intervention in my life. Many years later, my father told me that my mother had sent him letters stating that if he didn't take us back, she was going to put all of us in foster care. He also told me that he wished he had saved those letters, so he could show us why he took us in. Shortly after we arrived, he followed his usual playbook by disappearing with us and not letting our mother know where we were.

As a result, I went to a dozen different schools and did not hear from my mother for about seven years. She had me when she was around sixteen years old, so she was very immature in many ways. My father was constantly yelling at us, putting us down, and physically abusing us. I believe it was all due to his loneliness and anxiety of being a single parent, along with some physical and mental health issues. I honestly don't remember him ever being kind to us because those few instances where he was nice were overshadowed by the terror and the trauma he caused. It was horrible, and I cried almost every week.

It got so bad that one day, someone (I presume it was a neighbor) called the police and Child Protective Services. They came to our apartment and interviewed us several times. My father was there too, and they warned him about his abusive behavior. Michael was so scared that he told the social worker that my father only spanked him when he deserved it. I will never forget that lie. That was total baloney, but I did not blame him; he was just as scared as I was, and he was just one year older than me.

I told the child abuse investigator that he hit us all the time and showed them my scars and bruises. I asked them to make him stop and get us out of there as soon as possible. My father just gave me a mean and serious look while they were talking to me, like, "I am going to get you when they leave if you say anything." But he backed off for a while when the police showed up.

I was so glad they came that day because he had really crossed the line on multiple occasions. All I remember is crying from the pain and suffering. He would hit us with almost anything he could find: belts, brooms, extension cords, and we had marks on our bodies to prove it. He would hit us as hard as a grown man could swing, and it was very painful.

The police officers threatened my father and told him they were going to arrest him and take us away if he kept it up. I don't know who those neighbors were who called the authorities. It could have been the school district too, but whoever it was, we really appreciated it. Even though there were days when he did not hurt us or yell at us, he was not very friendly or nurturing, and we were scared most of the time.

I did my best to keep my distance and tried to stay out of his way and not look at him directly for any reason. We just never knew at what moment he was going to explode into a fury. It wasn't too bad in the daytime, when we were at school or at home alone, at least until he got home from work. We grew worried when it got close to five o'clock, because that's what time he would show up. When Christmas came, he never bought us any gifts and didn't even get us a Christmas tree. I remember feeling really sad because my mother always had a Christmas tree and gifts.

My brother, sister, and I grew up never ever hearing him say, "I love you," or even "Merry Christmas." Can you believe that? He was a real-life Scrooge, straight out of a Charles Dickens novel. I was embarrassed and felt ashamed when I went to school because all the kids would talk about the toys and gifts they got for Christmas, and he never got us anything. Can you imagine what that does to a little boy or little girl? When our birthdays came, there would be no birthday cake, presents, or celebration coming from him. It would just be another day, like he did not care, and this went on for many years. When someone would give us gifts, he would allow us to accept the gift in front of them, but then when he got angry, he would force us to throw them all away.

If you've ever been to Chicago, you know how hot and humid the summer gets and how cold the winters are. One day when I was about fourteen years old, my father got angry again and threw Michael and me out of the house, in the middle of a snowstorm.

This was the type of person my father was, and I believe it was due to his illness. Michael and I did not know where to go, so we sat together huddled next to a commercial office building a few blocks away, not knowing what we were going to do. We were out there in the snowstorm for a couple of hours, freezing. A neighbor saw us and called the police, who picked us up and took us home. The following day, my father was required to show up at a Child Abuse Prevention Office, where they interviewed him again and gave him another warning, saying that they were going to take us away from him.

When I left Chicago for the second and last time, my hands were literally shaking from all the trauma. Can you visualize this: a little boy's hands constantly shaking and trembling from the fear and suffering he was experiencing? One of my teachers at my elementary school called me into the office one day and wanted to know why my hands were shaking. They asked if everything was all right at home. I was afraid to say anything for fear of getting beaten again, so I just kept my mouth shut and did not say a word to them, as tears came down my eyes. I think my tears and silence said everything they needed to know. They may have been the ones who called the authorities, but I cannot be sure.

This was about the time when God intervened and started working on getting us out of there. I could not take any more abuse and wanted to end my life; I was at the point where life just wasn't worth living anymore, and I felt I was losing the will to live.

This was when I turned to God out of desperation, and this was when God first began to speak to me. The Bible says that the Lord God is a Father to the fatherless: "A father of the fatherless, a defender of widows, is God in His Holy habitation" (Psalm 68:5 NKJV). I began to pray to God to please help us; I believe my desperate prayers for help, along with my faith in God as a thirteen-year-old child, got His attention as I called upon His name.

I remember the Lord spoke to me one day when I was thirteen years old. He said to me, "Thus saith the LORD," and then showed me future events that would take place and reassured me that everything was going to be all right.

I thought to myself, *What kind of strange and funny English is that? "Thus saith the Lord"?* I wasn't even sure what that meant, except that He was speaking to me and reassuring me that everything was going to be okay. It would be many years later, when I was older and when I began to read the Bible, that I would once again see and hear those words. "Thus saith the Lord" comes right out of the Bible and signifies that God is about to say something important to you. The Lord God would speak through a prophet to give a message to a king, a person, or the leaders of a nation. God's message would always start with "Thus saith the Lord" (or "This is what God says"). You see, I had nowhere else to turn and nowhere to go; there was no mother around, and my father would not talk to me. I basically grew up like a fatherless child. He was constantly insulting me and putting me down, so I began to talk to God and pray to Him, and believe it or not, the Lord began to speak to me and comfort me at a very young age. God the Father began to answer some of my little prayers at the age of thirteen. Can you believe that?

Job 29:12 (NKJV) says, "Because I delivered the poor who cried out, the fatherless and the one who had no helper." My mother eventually found us again and called and said she wanted to take us back to California; my father agreed after he realized we had not seen our mother in almost a decade. We basically grew up without a mother and without a loving and nurturing father all those years. I think he knew deep down inside that it was too much for him to manage us kids alone; due to his state of mind, it may have overwhelmed him. I am sure he did the best he could under the circumstances and tried his best to play the role of a mother and father, but his efforts were not enough. I must, however, give my father credit for providing a roof over our heads and making sure we went to school, and he also made sure that we did not go hungry. The stress of being a single parent was a heavy burden on him, and it was not easy.

After we finally made it back to California, it took about three months for my hands to stop shaking.

> *As a father has compassion on his children, so the Lord has compassion on those who fear him.*

— Psalm 103:13 (NIV)

When I was ten years old, my father made a great decision he really needs to be given credit for: He placed us kids in a children's group home for about a year and half, while he got his life, finances, and circumstances together. It was called Lydia's Children's Home. There were other kids who also lived there; it was kind of like a boarding school. It turned out to be one of the best decisions my father made on our behalf. The people who ran the place took us everywhere, so we could experience new things, including going to church every Sunday.

I can honestly say that it was not only a relief to be there, but we had some of the most wonderful memories living there and made some great friends. Michael, Jacqueline, and I still talk about the good times we had there. I know now, looking in retrospect, that God softened my father's heart to place us there and helped him make the right choice; in the end, it was the best thing for all of us. This group home got us connected with our church and with the Christian families who would eventually pick us up and take us out to experience new things and also take us to their homes for the weekends and holidays.

Now let me tell you more about my other Father, the one who is also known as my heavenly Father. I was not completely aware that the Lord was with us during this ordeal, until I got older, had my encounter experience, and started to look back at the evidence. In fact, God the Father was there with us during the entire process and showed up to help, strengthen, and provide assistance for us when we needed it most.

When I was three and a half years old, I was taken away from my mother by the authorities, and it was for a good reason. Ana had me, as I mentioned, when she was only sixteen years old. She was a young girl from Nicaragua who could barely speak English. She did the best she could under the circumstances; however, she neglected us far too many times, which got the attention of the neighbors. For example, one day, I fell right down a sliding garbage disposal and landed in the apartment complex's trash container, with spaghetti all over me. She did not know where I was for about half an hour, until someone heard a little boy crying in the trash can and alerted her. She then went with a friend and pulled me out of it.

My mother worked all day and regularly left us kids in the apartment all alone. Not a really good idea, because something terrible could have happened to us, and one day, it almost did. Michael was about five, a year older than me; he decided to climb out the window of our second-story apartment and play on the fire escape's metal ladder. I followed right after him, not realizing the danger; can you imagine that? Someone saw two very young children playing on the fire escape and called the police. Thank God they did, or we could have fallen off and been killed.

Someone off the street shouted for us to get back in the house, so we did. The police eventually came and broke down the door of our apartment and then began speaking in a strange language I could not understand. That language, I would later find out, was English. Our mother only spoke to us in Spanish, so it was the first time I remember hearing another language. It sounded very strange to me, and the two men who came into the apartment were also dressed strangely. I did not know what police officers were at that time or why they wore uniforms.

I was hiding under the bed, eating toasted bread, when the police came in. They gathered all of us up and drove us to a juvenile detention facility. The officers were very nice to us, but it was still a terrifying experience, and as we drove away, I wasn't sure if I'd ever see my mother again.

I saw her that night at the juvenile detention facility, and she did not look happy. She had to work and could not always afford a babysitter, so she left us in the house alone that day. It didn't help that she was a young single mother, and as I mentioned, she only had a fourth grade education. She had come from Nicaragua as a young girl, fleeing an oppressive country with a brutal dictatorship that had imprisoned members of her family.

I was left at the juvenile detention center because, according to the doctors who examined me, I had some questionable marks and bruises on my body. The state took custody and did not return me to my mother. I waited in that facility for over six months until a family came and picked me up. I spent the next several years living with the Martin family, who were very loving and provided a stable and healthy environment. Anita and Don Martin are still my parents and family until today, and I still call them Mom and Dad. You see, this was the first time God intervened in my life; working on my behalf, He separated me from my birth mother at a very young age in order to place me in a stable, safe, and healthy home.

I learned how to speak English, went to a private Catholic school, and learned about God. When I was about to turn four years old, my foster mother, Anita Martin, asked me what I wanted for my birthday. According to her, I said I wanted a birthday party with a cake and a Mass. So they called the priest of our local parish and arranged a simple church Mass service at my house, followed by the birthday party. Because I was sent to this foster home by the state, Anita was also given a check every month for taking care of me, and she made sure that I had the best clothes and nice shoes, lots of toys, great food, and most importantly, a loving family. I was very happy.

However, this would only last a few years. My biological mother and my grandmother demanded that my foster parents return me to them, and they eventually got their way because they worked with a social worker and threatened legal action. Anita was broken-hearted the day I left, and so was I. She offered to adopt me, but my mother refused. Anita ended up grieving over me for the next ten years and wondered what happened to me.

I was eventually reunited with my foster mother many years later, exactly as she saw it in a dream I believe God had given her. Anita had a recurring dream that one day, I would come back home to her, and a decade later, it happened exactly as she had dreamed.

After I was returned to my biological mother, I lived with her for just a few short months before she sent Michael and me back to live with our father in Chicago.

My heavenly Father was continuously active in my life, in subtle ways I could barely detect. When I look back at all the tough times, I can clearly see His footprints and evidence of His hand at work. For example, when my father refused to celebrate Christmas and get us a Christmas tree and gifts, the Lord worked miracles around this problem. Another family from our church who was assigned to be my prayer parents found a way for us to have a happy holiday.

Somehow, they heard that my father did not celebrate the holidays and that we never got a chance to have a Christmas, so they picked us up and invited us over to their home for the holidays and other occasions. Michael, Jacqueline, and I got a chance to experience a real Christmas with a Christmas tree and gifts. When you're a little kid, believe me, that's a big deal. We would spend a few days in their house with their two boys, who were our age. It was so much fun and one of the happiest times I can remember. God was doing this for us right in the middle of all the turmoil and chaos. They picked us up from time to time throughout the year and took us for the weekend.

We experienced God's love, faithfulness, and mercy through this Christian family. The Lord was constantly sending us people to pick us up, bring us to church, and take us out to do new things and go new places. These church people did nice things for us, even celebrating our birthday with gifts; this was something my father never did, but I must give him some credit for allowing someone else to do it for us. When my father threw Michael and me out into a winter snowstorm that night, I know it was the Lord who got our neighbor out of bed in the middle of the night and had him go for walk in just the right direction where he would find us huddled together, freezing. That was not an accident that we were found; on the contrary, I know now that it was a divine appointment to save our lives.

You see, as I look back at these hard times, I can see the footprints of Almighty God saving, healing, and delivering us from one thing after another. My father, as I mentioned, was not well and would regularly punish us with his bare hands, but one day, he went to work at the steel factory, and the hand he hit us with got injured in one of the machines he used. He was required to get stitches and surgery; he was in a lot of pain and was not able to use that hand to hurt us again for a long time.

I knew instinctively that God had allowed his hand to be injured so he would stop using it to hurt us. My father, who clearly had anger management issues, was experiencing a form of karma, or as the Bible says, a sowing and reaping effect: the pain and suffering he caused with those hands was coming back to him now.

Here's a funny story about this incident: One day, while my father's hand was fresh out of surgery, he got angry again and ran across the room to punish us, but miraculously, he slipped right before he reached us and landed on his injured hand. He was cursing and crying out in great pain as he tried to get off the floor. It was revealed to me that God sent His angel to stop him right before he reached us and caused him to stumble, slip, and fall on the injured hand so that he wouldn't hurt us. He was then in double pain, both from landing on his hand and from the humiliation of falling before us. We quietly laughed, but God let me know personally that His divine presence was at work; He intervened to protect us from another unnecessary beating.

My father became so frustrated that he left us alone, and I think he also knew deep down inside that the fall was divinely orchestrated to protect us, so he backed off in fear. I got to see this

in time to forgive my father (who was also abused as a child) for everything he did to my mother and to us. When I asked the Lord why He allowed this to happen to us, He revealed to me in my prayer time that my father was not well; he suffered a lot from various things and also had a hard life growing up, and it was not easy for him. My father was given a certain number of years to raise his own children and get it right, but he failed in the process, then the Lord removed us from his life for good.

The Lord also showed me that He would use my experience for His glory someday. He revealed to me that I was like His precious gold, being refined and forged in a furnace of fire so that He could mold, perfect, and strengthen my character. One day, He would use me for some greater purpose, perhaps like writing this book for you. I had every reason to be bitter and hate my father, and I wanted deeply to settle a score with him, but as I got older, I chose the right path, which was to forgive him and be reconciled with him. God had given me the strength, maturity, and power, through our Lord and Savior Jesus Christ and His precious Holy Spirit, to forgive him; it's something I could not have done alone.

One day, the Lord touched my heart that it was time to call my father and let him know I was coming to see him. It had been twenty years since I had heard from him, and I was now in my thirties. So I went down to Puerto Rico, where he lived, and saw him personally and forgave him. He told me that his behavior was due to stress, anxiety, loneliness, and his mental illness, and that he had been missing us terribly for many years and had regretted what he had done. He also told me that he experienced the consequences for his behavior and that God had dealt with him severely. He lost his whole family and had additional health problems shortly afterwards. Somewhere in our absence and in his time of suffering and testing, he had given his life to the Lord and was now a changed man.

I just forgave him and let it go, because it was the right thing to do. I know that my other Father, God the Father, the one who looked out for me and raised me into a good, strong, and honorable young man, was very pleased.

> *I have read the last page of the Bible. It's all going to turn out all right.*

—Billy Graham

Chapter 8

My Prayer Formula for Success: A Guide for Getting Your Prayers Answered

Ask, and it will be given to you; seek, and you will find; knock, and it will be opened to you. For everyone who asks receives, and he who seeks finds, and to him who knocks it will be opened.

—Matthew 7:7–8 (NASB)

As I mentioned, the Lord God Almighty has answered just about every prayer I've ever asked, from getting me through college to helping me find a spouse, start a family, and set up my business. He will answer your prayers too, when you learn to live a life surrendered and committed to Him. All my prayers were answered in one way or another, especially the ones that involved big life changes and critical decisions that affected my future. Some were answered quickly, and others took a little longer, and some were answered in a way I was not expecting or anticipating; however, just about all of them have been answered. There are many techniques and methods that can work for getting your prayers answered, but this is the one I personally use, and it has worked for me wonderfully.

I'd like to share with you my personal prayer formula the Lord taught me over the years, for getting your prayers and requests answered so that things you've been hoping for and believing in will begin to materialize for you. It does not matter what the request is, for the most part; however, it should be in accordance with His will and divine plan. Keep in mind that when you do pray, you must be pragmatic; don't ask for things that are ridiculous, evil, or trivial, or things that will separate you from God's love and purpose for your life. He will definitely not answer those prayers. For example, if you are a sixteen-year-old kid, don't ask the Lord God for a red Ferrari convertible, because even if you did get it, you probably could not afford the insurance or the maintenance and repairs, so please be practical.

Instead, you may want to ask the Lord God for a nice car that you can afford to maintain so you can enjoy going out and for getting to school or work on time. Also, if you don't have a job, it's probably not a good idea to ask the Lord for a spouse just yet. First, get your life in order, where you have the capacity to take care of yourself, and this will put you in the position to be able to take care of someone else and support a family. In this case, I would first ask Him to help you get through school or help you get a job, so you can begin to take care of yourself and save some money for the future. Also, you will need to be at a certain maturity level to handle a relationship.

Just be practical when you pray for things. God takes no pleasure in listening to foolish, outlandish, or trivial requests.

> *But seek first the kingdom of God and His righteousness,*
> *and all these things shall be added [or given] to you.*
>
> — Matthew 6:33 (NKJV)

The first step to getting your prayers answered quickly is to be in a right relationship with the Lord God Almighty. This means you need to be seeking Him and His kingdom so that you can begin to walk in His power. You can do that by applying the techniques I've outlined for you in the previous chapters. Let's review: First and foremost, the Lord needs to be hearing from you regularly, so you need to be praying to Him each week and developing a personal and intimate relationship with Him.

Second, you are being watched and observed, and everything you do is being recorded in His book by His angels, so make sure you are spending some quality time each week in His manual. He needs to see you reading His Word, the Bible, and working toward understanding and obeying Him and His principles. When you honor Him, He will honor you and begin to bless you and answer your requests.

Third, make sure throughout your day and week that you are fixing you heart and mind on Him through meditation; this way, you stay focused and don't get discouraged. Fourth, make sure you are working on your character each week and also attending a house of worship. Fifth, be a pure vessel that He can use to make an impact in your arena of influence or the community where you live. In other words, avoid sinful behavior and be open to reaching out to those God sends your way. He has strategically placed you in a certain area where you can reach specific people around you; it's no accident you are in that neighborhood, office, workplace, school, or area: It's all been divinely orchestrated, whether you're aware of it or not. There are no accidents with God.

Once these basic steps are checked off, which is very easy to do, you can now begin to apply the prayer technique. Keep in mind that prayer coupled with fasting has an even stronger effect, when you're ready for that level of commitment. When you pray, you must be sincere, pray from the heart, activate your faith, and be persistent. Here is a parable of a widow who finally got her prayer request answered through perseverance and patience.

The Parable of the Persistent Widow

In a certain town there was a judge who neither feared God nor cared what people thought. And there was a widow in that town who kept coming to him with the plea, "Grant me justice against my adversary." For some time he refused. But finally he said to himself, "Even though I don't fear God or care what people think, yet because this widow keeps bothering me, I will see that she gets justice, so that she won't eventually come and attack me!"

(Luke 18:2–5 NIV)

Activate Your Faith

He [Jesus] replied, "Because you have so little faith. Truly I tell you, if you have faith as small as a mustard seed, you can say to this mountain, 'Move from here to there,' and it will move. Nothing will be impossible for you.

(Matthew 17:20 NIV)

Here are two prayer techniques I use for getting my prayers answered:

The Lord's Prayer

> *Our Father which art in heaven, Hallowed be Thy*
> *Name. Thy kingdom come, Thy will be done in earth,*
> *as it is in heaven. Give us this day our daily bread.*
> *And forgive us our debts, as we forgive our debtors.*
> *And lead us not into temptation, but deliver us from*
> *evil: for thine is the kingdom, and the power, and the*
> *glory, for ever. Amen.*
>
> — Matthew 6:9–13 (KJV)

My Personal Prayer Method

A great way you can start the prayer is by saying these words: "I call upon the name of the Lord God Almighty." (The Names of God section is also a great resource.)

I encourage you to get familiar with the other names of God and use those names when you pray. I always do, and this will definitely get His ear and His attention.

1. Begin your prayer by calling upon the name of the Lord and thanking and praising Him for who He is and for giving you the wonderful gift of life. Thank Him for being your Creator and heavenly Father. Lift up His name. Reading the Psalms will give you some great examples of how to pray. He is a great and mighty God who likes to be praised, acknowledged, and thanked. (Take a few minutes right now to do this.)

2. Next, thank God for all the blessings that you do have. Take personal inventory of the blessings you've been given: food on the table, a roof over your head, a place to live, good

health, a warm sweater, a vehicle to get around in, a job, a best friend, parents, a pet, and so on. Take inventory each week and count your blessings. Show the Lord that you are grateful for what you do have and are willing to patiently wait for the other things to come to you in their due season. It's important to have an attitude of gratitude. (Take a few minutes to do this right now.)

3. Next, repent and ask God to forgive you for anything you may have said, thought, or done to offend or hurt someone the past week, month, or year. Repent daily and ask the Lord to forgive you of trespasses and sinful behavior. Ask Him to help you forgive others. Also, if there is anyone in your life you have a grudge against or have not forgiven (it does not matter whose fault it was), ask the Lord to help you be mature enough to forgive them. Be the bigger person or the adult in the room; let it go, and move on. Otherwise, your heavenly Father won't forgive you, and your prayers may go unanswered: "that your prayers may not be hindered" (1 Peter 3:7 NKJV). Maybe it's an ex-partner or former coworker or boss or family member or friend. If you are struggling to forgive them, then ask God to divinely intervene and help you forgive them and let it go. You might not be able to do it without His help. (Take a few minutes to do this.)

And whenever you stand praying, if you have anything against anyone, forgive him, that your Father in heaven may also forgive you your trespass. But if you do not forgive, neither will your Father in heaven forgive your trespasses.

— Mark 11:25–26 (NKJV)

4. Next, pray for other people who have a need or are having a difficult time. Maybe it's an ambulance that drove by you this day or a neighbor who's having financial problems or someone you know in trouble; perhaps it's a family member, a stranger, a homeless person, someone in jail, or your government officials. You can always find someone to pray for. Ask God to open your heart to others who need His assistance, so you can pray for them. Praying for others shows the God of heaven that you are selfless and not selfish and that you genuinely care and are thinking about others and not just yourself. (Take a few minutes to do this.)

5. Next, pray and ask the Lord to continue to mold and perfect your character into the godly person He wants you to become. He is the potter, and we are the clay: "But now, O Lord, you are our Father; we are the clay, and You our potter; And all we are the work of Your hand" (Isaiah 64:8 NKJV). A Christlike character is the ultimate goal. Being honorable, righteous, loving, forgiving, and a person of integrity are great things to petition and ask for. (Take a few minutes to do this.)

6. Finally, slip in at the end whatever you want, or whatever you request, and patiently wait for the answered prayer. It will be answered. Some prayers will be answered right away; others will be answered at the right time and season. What is important is not to lose hope; keep trusting and thanking God for the answered prayer, no matter how small the blessing. Activate your faith and rest in peace knowing that the prayer is being answered, and it's on the way. Don't doubt God; just believe and trust Him.

7. Now—and this is extremely important, what I am about to say—quote this scripture below as you ask for the request and believe in your heart that you are receiving the answered prayer. I usually end the prayer by saying, "I thank you that it is done," and then I visualize it coming to pass. Do not

doubt in your heart, as the scripture says, but believe you are receiving it. Thank Him in advance for the answered prayer, and you will receive an answer to your request, but remember; it will be in God's time. Also, if you can find someone to pray with you and agree with you in prayer, this also helps tremendously to speeds things up. You will find prayer partners in a house of worship in your community. This is another good reason to get into a good church as soon as possible, if you don't have one.

And you can end each prayer by saying, "I thank you in the Mighty Name of Jesus."
Here are some great scriptures you can quote as you pray:

Therefore I say to you, whatever things you ask when you pray, believe that you receive them, and you will have them.

— Mark 11:24 (NKJV)

And whatever things you ask in prayer, believing, you will receive.

— Matthew 21:22 (NKJV)

Now you can pray this list in any order you like; however, this is the method I have learned over the years that works the best for me. Do this every time you pray. Keep pressing on and waiting until the prayer is answered. There are other great scriptures you can quote, but these are a great starting point. The average person does not realize this, but the Bible is like a treasure chest filled with secret golden passages you can use in time of need and in prayer for your health and personal benefit. You just need to do your homework by going on a treasure hunt and finding them. When the scriptures are prayed out loud, they are like secret combination codes. Once they are spoken, similar to a voice activation mechanism, you can use them to unlock heaven and whatever it is you are hoping for, in accordance with God's will.

However, your godly character needs to be intact in order to have access to heaven. I would also keep a prayer journal of all the prayers God has answered for you. This is important, because it will help you remember what God did for you in the past, and this will help encourage you in the future when you are going through something difficult, facing a new challenge, or waiting for another prayer to be answered. It's unbelievable how fast people will forget the miracles God does for them; this is why it's important to keep a prayer journal and meditate regularly on all the things He has done for you and answered over the years.

Keep in mind that sometimes God will answer a prayer with a no, and you need to be okay with that. He may have something better for you, instead. He is really looking out for your best interest. In other words, He does not always give me a parking spot in front; sometimes, I have to walk a block or two, because He might just be testing my commitment level to Him. In the end, we serve Him for who He is, not for what we can get out of Him.

As I mentioned earlier, God is not a genie in a bottle to give you whatever you want, whenever you want it. More importantly, He is there to give you what is best for you and always at the right time. He is looking out for you; He cares greatly about you and your purpose in life and wants to make sure you fulfill your destiny. The Lord will give you what you desire the most: "He shall give thee the desires of thine heart" (Psalm 37:4 KJV). More importantly, He knows what is best for you at each pivotal point and stage in your life.

Keep in mind that not everything that looks good is good for you, no matter how it makes you feel; not all that glitters is gold. I found that out the hard way, so you must always trust Him, no matter how He answers your prayer; He knows what's best for you and what will make you happy in the end. He actually knows you better than you know yourself; this is a good reason why you should trust Him always, no matter what happens to you in your life.

The everlasting God is always concerned about your health, safety, and well-being, so your prayers will be answered according to His will and divine plan. He loves you too much to see you suffer and be set back for years by foolish choices or trivial requests. The Lord will always answer the most important prayers impacting your life in a big way; however, one of the main reasons He will not give you every little thing you think you want or ask for is because He is your heavenly Father, not your sugar daddy.

> *Prayer is putting oneself in the hands of God.*
>
> —Mother Teresa

A Wedding Day Request and the Arrival of a Special Guest

> *Be anxious for nothing, but in everything by prayer and supplication, with thanksgiving, let your requests be made known to God.*
>
> —Philippians 4:6 (NKJV)

Before I tell you what special circumstance happened on the day I got married, I would like to share with you how I met my wife. I had been praying for a wife for about eight years and was doing the best I could to remain patient, sanctified, and ready for this level of commitment. I prayed to the Lord and asked if He would send me His choice for my life when He felt I was ready for it because, as I had found out through my past experiences, I was not good at picking the right girls. I always seemed to select the wrong ones who were not ideally suited for me. As a result, these relationships would end in a breakup, or us not getting along, or just remaining friends. People typically pick what looks good on the outside, but God also looks at the heart. For some reason, I felt like this was never going to happen for me, but I just kept praying, believing, waiting, and trusting God.

Then one day while I was at work, shortly after my foster father died, a young lady came into the bank where I was working to open an account. Rose had a lovely smile and looked like a natural, wholesome country girl, with a sweet personality. It was a riveting moment for me, and I really felt drawn to her. I helped her open her accounts; however, we did not say much to each other and kept our conversation limited to our business at the bank. I should note that she had come into the bank with someone else, so I tried to be as respectful and professional as possible by not engaging in too much conversation.

After Rose left, I did not see her again for over a year. However, she had made quite an impression on me, so much so that I began to pray and ask the Lord to please send me someone like her. I never prayed for Rose specifically, but I did keep mentioning her name to the Lord and asked if He could send me someone kind of like her. I prayed this way for well over a year and a half.

Then one day, she came in again, and this time she was alone. She needed help with her accounts and was very friendly toward me. As I was updating her profile, she told me a little bit about her life, including where she worked. She invited me to come down to the store where she worked. On my day off, I went to visit her and picked up a few things; I smiled at her once I saw her, said hello, and then left. It took me a few more visits until I built up the courage to ask her out; then one day, I asked her if she wanted to go to lunch, and she said yes.

Well, the rest is history; we hit it off very well and were married a few years later. I would also like to mention that one day while I was at work, she brought me a plate of food that she had prepared at home. I had not asked her to make me anything; she just brought it over, and it was so good that I said to myself, *I'd have to be crazy or insane to let this girl pass me by.* That great and wonderful cooking, combined with her lovely personality and character, were the primary things that convinced me that this girl was a keeper.

But I also want to tell you that after Rose and I decided to get married and we got engaged, we did not move into the same apartment or live together until after the wedding. I did not want to start out our new life this way because it would not be pleasing to God. Rose's parents and family appreciated that I felt this way and was putting God's principles first in my life.

Back to the story of my wedding day: We had hired a wedding planner to help manage everything, and it took two years to make all the preparations. I had asked the Lord in prayer, throughout the year, to please bless the wedding and all the plans leading up to that date. We had selected May 25 as the day, and I also asked the Lord to please remember to come on this day. I prayed, "You are invited, heavenly Father and Lord Jesus, and You are my special guests; please don't forget May 25 is the day." I said this prayer well over a hundred times during the two years as I was preparing for the wedding.

When our wedding day finally arrived, I was extremely busy meeting people and thanking friends, family members, and guests. I was also busy taking photographs, tasting food, and checking all the arrangements. I had completely forgotten about my request for the Lord to show up at my wedding, because I was too preoccupied and was having such a grand time. Everything was just perfect and ran smoothly. The ceremony and the rest of the scheduled events went flawlessly with no problems. Then suddenly, at around seven o'clock, when I began to slow dance with my foster mother, the most unusual thing happened.

Anita looked at me, kind of like in a daze, and said, "Son, I don't know what just happened, but I feel like I am dreaming."

I felt it too; as we were dancing, I felt like I was in a dream. It was like an intense, dreamy state of consciousness of some sort, but I was awake. I noticed that the entire atmosphere had changed a few minutes before we began to dance. It was almost as if everyone in the room was in a dream or a trance. There was something magical in the air, and it filled the room. It all felt very mysterious and supernatural. The best way to describe what I was experiencing is the following: It felt like I could breathe underwater. This is one way I can explain it to you. The air felt different, like it had a density that I could feel, sort of like a muggy day when there is humidity and there is heavy water vapor in the air.

It was surreal, almost as if some form of spiritual substance or some kind of vibrational energy had filled the air and permeated the room. Rose also said she felt like she was in dream and like she was walking on clouds. Other people said similar things. Shortly after the mother-and-son dance was over, I had about seven or eight people, of all different ages ranging from eighteen to eighty, come up to me and tell me they felt like they were sleepwalking or dreaming.

One individual told me, "I know I am awake, but I feel like I am dreaming."

Someone else asked, "Am I really here, and is this all really happening?"

Then I realized, by the time the last person mentioned this to me, what was happening. The Lord of Glory, our heavenly Father, had come to the wedding. You see, He was invited and was making His presence known all around the room and wedding hall. None of these people knew how to interpret His arrival. You could feel His overwhelming presence, power, and love everywhere. It was remarkable; it made just about everyone feel like they were in some kind of a hypnotic dream, and time itself appeared to slow down.

It was one of the most extraordinary things I have ever experienced. The spiritual energy in the air made you feel like you were living in a fairy tale, like a classic Disney movie. I am doing my best to describe to you the sensation because it was truly magical and unbelievable in nature, and I will never forget it. The "dream-like state," as some people were calling it, lasted for about an hour and then faded away. I cannot tell you exactly how many people experienced this phenomenon, but I can say that almost everyone in the room who talked to me was affected and touched in one way or another. People afterwards were coming up to me saying, it was the best wedding they had ever experienced.

Others said, "You really know how to throw a party."

One person said, "You must have spent a fortune on your wedding," but of course we did not because we were on a limited budget. By the way, if you're thinking somebody spiked the punch, they did not: We did not have any alcohol or punch at our wedding. When I asked various people what they liked the most about the wedding, they all said the same thing. I personally cannot tell you what I liked most, one way or another, because every part of it was just perfect. Now, I did not see the Lord in any visible way with my eyes, and He did not speak to me, but His holy presence and supernatural power were palpable everywhere. When God truly shows up, you will feel like you are in a dream; that's how spectacular and disorienting His power can be. It kind of leaves you in a daze or, as these people described it, in a dream state. You see, I had completely forgotten that I had personally invited Him over a hundred times during the last couple of years, but the Lord did not forget that date, May 25, so when He did show up in His power and glory, I was not ready for it. It was truly amazing because honestly, I never imagined He would actually take the time to come to an average person's wedding.

In fact, the pastor who presided over our ceremony told me afterwards that he had done seventeen weddings that year and said, "Your wedding was very special, Luis. God's presence was definitely there, and it was the one wedding which stood out from the rest."

If you're wondering how all this was possible, you need to know that all I really did was just invite Him through a prayer; that's it. I would like to close by saying that if you are thinking about getting married or finding someone special to share your life with, then don't forget to ask God who His choice is for your life. He just may surprise you with someone unexpected and wonderful. Also, when you're sending out your invitations, please don't forget to invite the most important person of all besides your spouse, family, and friends, and that's your heavenly Father. He just may take you up on your offer and show up at your wedding too.

The Drunk Driver and God's Hedge of Protection

He shall cover you with His feathers, and under His wings you shall take refuge; His truth shall be your shield and buckler.

—Psalm 91:4 (NKJV)

Walking with God and trusting Him for his protection is similar to getting great insurance for your home, vehicle, property, or business, and making an investment in that policy. Let me explain what I mean: when you faithfully pay your monthly premiums, the insurance carrier guarantees that you're covered in case of an unexpected accident or unfortunate event. You just never know when something is going to happen. When something bad does happen, you're relieved to know that you're covered for the loss. And that gives you peace of mind. I've been in a few car accidents, and my insurance provider took care of everything, including the rental of my replacement vehicle, whether it was my fault or not. I was glad I had the policy in place and that I paid my monthly premium on time because on the day of the unforeseen event, I was covered. Walking with God and trusting Him for is protection is similar in many ways.

I would like to tell you a short story about God's grace and His protection. When I got married, I bought Rose a new car as a wedding gift. The car she wanted was a white Volkswagen Passat.

Because the vehicle was new, and I was making payments on it, I was required to get full coverage. One night a year later, while Rose was on her way home, she was at a stop light, waiting for it to turn green. It was about eight o'clock, and Julius Maximus, our son, who was about ten months old at the time, was sleeping in his car seat. I had repeatedly told her she should not be on the phone when she drove our son around. He was my first-born child, and I was always concerned about his well-being. She was pretty good about not being on the phone with the child in the car, but this night, I guess it was important to take the call, so she was talking on the phone.

As a result, she did not see this drunk driver coming straight at her from behind. He was going about 50 miles per hour, and he hit her car very hard. Her car was completely destroyed from the back end, and Julius was at the center of the impact. Thank goodness she had put a blanket over the baby's car seat. The drunk driver almost killed them, but by God's good grace, they were saved. The Lord covered them with His feathers, and they took refuge under His wings. All the shattered glass fell on top of the baby blanket surrounding my son's car seat but did not penetrate the blanket or cut him in any way.

Rose called me in panic; she was crying and screaming on the phone that she had been in an accident. I asked nervously how the baby was and was praying and hoping that she would not tell me that he had been killed. She told me that he was okay, but that he was a little shaken up. I was greatly relieved. "Thank you, Lord," I said. I got down to the scene of the accident in about fifteen minutes. I left the house so fast that I forgot to put on a pair of pants and ran out with just some running shorts I had on.

When I arrived, she was crying and in terrible pain as the paramedics were putting her on a stretcher and taking her into the ambulance. She kept saying that she could not breathe, and she appeared to be in shock. She would later tell me that she did not remember me being in the ambulance with her at all. After the paramedic checked her over, I asked if she was going to be okay. He said that he didn't know and couldn't be sure.

A few minutes later, the paramedic said something to me that sent a cold chill down my spine, words I will never forget. It was a very sobering moment. As I asked the paramedic again if she was going to be all right, he looked at me directly and said these frightful words to me: "I am not sure if your wife is going to live or even make it to the hospital."

I don't know what caused him to reach that conclusion, but somehow, when he was checking her vitals and pulse, he made that determination. Maybe he saw death coming in her eyes; I can't be sure, but after looking at the accident and seeing the damage to the car, he may have been convinced of his diagnosis. I asked if I could ride with her in the ambulance to the hospital, a request he granted.

I also asked him if it was okay if I prayed for her along the way, and he said, "That's fine; go ahead pray for her."

He looked very serious and worried about her condition. I was not about to let my wife die. I said to myself that I would do everything in my power to help her. Before I prayed for her, I called my mother and was glad she answered the phone. I told her that Rose was involved in a car accident and explained that she was hit by a drunk driver and that the paramedic told me that she may not live. I asked my mother to please drop whatever she was doing and pray right now, and then I got off the phone.

I remember being afraid that Rose might die en route to the hospital. I decided to activate my faith and trust God. I began to pray out loud, nonstop, from the moment they took her into the ambulance to the moment they rushed her into the hospital's emergency room. As I mentioned, Rose does not recall me being in the ambulance with her. I remember asking God not to let her die and reminded Him that we had only been married a year and that the baby needs his mother. I petitioned God to save her life and asked the Lord to operate on her right then and heal her completely. She was not bleeding, but I didn't know what broken bones or internal damage she may have sustained. I prayed passionately and pleaded with the God of heaven to intervene immediately.

Although it was less than a fifteen-minute ride to the hospital, it seemed like an eternity as I listened to the sirens screaming in the background. When we got to the ER, the doctors frantically began to check her over with various machines, diagnostic equipment, and x-rays. The doctors also examined Julius. I was all alone, waiting to find out news about her condition and silently continued to pray. She was calm when they finally brought her back to her room. I stayed at her side for an hour, still praying and wondering what the doctors were going to tell me, and honestly, I expected the worst.

Then, to my great surprise, a doctor came into her room and said that she was going to be fine and that she had no internal bleeding, broken bones, or whiplash, not even a concussion. In fact, they said, she was perfectly fine, and she could go home in an hour. We were both amazed by the doctor's report. Her car had been destroyed, but my son and Rose were fine. They came away from that wreck literally without a scratch. Can you believe that? Now when I look at the photos of that car, I can't imagine how that's possible. But I know what the Bible says: that with God, all things are possible. I routinely pray for God to place a hedge of protection around my family at all times. It's a scripture I learned many years ago; it's found in Job 1:9–10 (NKJV): "So Satan answered the Lord and said, 'Does Job fear God for nothing? Have You not made a hedge around him, around his household, and around all that he has on every side?'" I truly believe that when I prayed to God to not let her die and asked the Lord to fix whatever was wrong with her, He answered my prayer and began to work on her at that moment.

I did not see any visible signs of a miracle at work; however, I did feel that God was doing something with her, which I could not see with my natural eyes. I will probably never know until I get to heaven what God did to save her life that day, but I do know, after looking at the condition of the vehicle, that He definitely intervened and did something for her. You just don't walk away from an accident like that without a scratch.

As we left the hospital together, I remember saying to Rose, "I am so glad we went to church this past Sunday to honor God, and I am glad I left my offering." You see, God showed up at that unexpected accident and protected our family and covered us under His insurance policy, according to those verses in the Bible.

A few days later, after the insurance adjuster looked at the vehicle, the company wrote me a check because they decided the car was not repairable and declared it a total loss. Like the insurance company that covered the vehicle that day, God will also protect you in times of uncertainty, just like that scripture in Psalm 91:4 says above when you learn to walk with Him.

The Nuclear Option and a Miraculous Recovery

> *For I will restore health to you, and heal you of your wounds, says the Lord.*
>
> —Jeremiah 30:17 (NKJV)

When Julius my son was three years old, he became very ill and would not eat anything for five days. It's every parent's nightmare when their child is injured or ill. On the third day, we brought him to the emergency room at Stanford Hospital and had a doctor examine him. The physician recommended the usual basic treatment: have him get plenty of rest and give him plenty of liquids, and then he gave us instructions, which included kid's vitamins and protein drink supplements to help him until he was ready to eat, along with a few other recommendations. The doctor said that if his condition did not get any better, to bring him back in a couple of days.

On the seventh day, I became worried and a little frightened because he did not appear to be getting better but worse. His face by now had become pale white; he had no desire to talk and could barely walk, staggering like a drunken person when he tried to do so. I could not sleep at night or concentrate at work because I was preoccupied with his condition; I was not sure what to do or why he was sick. So we made the arrangements to take him back to the hospital that day. At this point, I got very angry and said, "Enough is enough. That's it; since nothing appears to be working, I am going to use the nuclear option and nuke this problem and whatever is making him sick."

I called Susan, a friend who is considered by many to be a prayer warrior and who is a woman of great and incredible faith; she loves to pray for hours. When she answered the phone, I told her that I had a serious problem; Julius was very sick and weak and had not eaten anything in almost a week; his face had turned completely pale, and honestly, I was scared.

I asked, "Can you pray with me right now? This cannot wait, and I cannot afford to see his health decline any further. Let's ask God to touch him right now and heal him and petition the Lord to intervene before he gets any worse."

I asked her to get into agreement with me and let's nuke this problem and illness with a barrage of prayers and fasting. I quoted every scripture I knew on healing and deliverance as I prayed, and then I asked her to pray and do the same. We prayed passionately and with great fervor for about fifteen minutes straight and then ended the prayer by thanking God and trusting Him for my child's recovery. I specially asked the Lord to give him a voracious appetite to eat and a new desire for all proteins (for some reason, he did not want to eat any kind of meat).

I was hoping that we'd see a turnaround in his condition within the next few days. However, within an hour of us praying together, his grandmother called to say that Julius had asked for something to eat. She told me that he suddenly just snapped out of it and was requesting all kinds of things to eat. He appeared to be extremely hungry now. I would like to note that this was also the first time he requested a cheeseburger, something he had never eaten before up to this point.

I thought to myself, *Well, I did ask the Lord to give him a voracious appetite and desire for meat.* I was so happy that tears filled my eyes; I thanked the Lord for His divine intervention on my son's behalf. Relieved that he was now eating and would be getting better, I could now get back to work and take care of my other responsibilities. Julius went on to make a quick and miraculous recovery and has not been sick like that since. Skeptics do not understand the power of prayer, but it does work for those who believe and walk with God. I have seen its power first-hand, the supernatural in action; you just need to active your faith and call upon the name of the Lord. Through this experience, I realized that God has given all parents the responsibility, power, and authority to pray over their children. He will answer those prayers on their behalf, especially during a time of need and when it concerns their safety, health, and well-being. I would like to close by reminding all parents to pray for their children regularly. These are prayers that God will definitely answer.

Chapter 9

> *Those who walk with God always reach their destination.*
>
> —Henry Ford

I went to business school and graduated with a bachelor's in general management and an MBA. However, I am going to share with you something they don't teach in business school regarding generating phenomenal sales and bringing in customers and new business. I am going to let you in on an ancient secret you may find useful. I discovered an amazing passage in the Bible I have been using for many years that has helped me exponentially in business and sales. I was shown this scripture and the revelation of how it works one day while I was praying and doing my daily devotion. My life has never been the same, and the secret can be found in the book of Deuteronomy.

And you shall remember the Lord your God, for it is He who gives you power to get wealth, that He may establish His covenant which He swore to your fathers, as it is this day.

— Deuteronomy 8:18 (NKJV)

For many years, I was involved in sales while working in retail management and in banking, selling financial services. I was an average salesperson until I learned this mysterious technique. Once I began applying this spiritual principle, I was able to become number one in sales and service. My district manager, supervisors, and colleagues were scratching their heads in surprise and could not figure out how I was doing it; however, it was not me doing it alone, but God doing it through me. I will share with you the secret behind that success, so you can apply it yourself and see that it really does work.

In business school, they teach how you can become successful by utilizing various business plans, models, and methods. Some of these ideas include knowing your product, understanding your competitors and customer needs, developing a great mission statement, differentiating your product or service, being aware of your strengths and weaknesses, delegating responsibilities, and applying various marketing strategies (e.g., being first to market, advertising, using strategic planning, selecting the ideal location, leveraging finances, and sharing referrals).

These are all great tools to make sales and generate business for yourself and your company, and I encourage you to use them; they do work. However, they are limited in scope and don't guarantee you will attain the number one position in your office. If you truly desire to be the best in sales at your company and want success to flow right to you so you can be a leader in your industry, then all you need to do is quote, apply, and pray this special and magical scripture found in the book of Deuteronomy.

> *The Lord will open to you His good treasure, the heavens, to give the rain to your land in its season, and to bless all the work of your hand. You shall lend to many nations, but you shall not borrow. And the Lord will make you the head and not the tail; you shall be above only, and not be beneath, if you heed the commandments of the Lord your God, which I command you today, and are careful to observe them.*

— Deuteronomy 28:12–13 (NKJV)

All you need to do is pray this scripture daily before you begin your work day, fulfill your job description to your employer, and maintain a godly character. You might be thinking that this is too good to be true, and it really is, without God's help. You see, either the Bible is telling the truth or it's not. I already figured out the answer to that question. This may sound hard to believe, but before you're tempted to dismiss this idea, I encourage you to give it a try. What do you have to lose? The only way to find out if it really does work is to give it a shot. As I have discovered, it's one of the best-kept secrets, and it's reserved for those who walk upright with God.

Keep in mind that trusting God for any of His promises is always going to be a walk of faith. All you need to do is give it a try, and you will see that I am telling you the truth. My district manager once said that prayer was not an option. But I am here to tell you that prayer is always my first option and my last option, especially whenever I take on a large project or am confronted with a big work challenge.

God is promising to make you number one in your position. He will also open the heavens for you along with His good treasure and will bless the work of your hands, which includes blessing just about everything you do. He says that He Himself will make you the head (top or first) and not the tail (bottom or last). You don't even have to worry about striving to become number one in sales or being a leader at your office; that's not your problem to worry about, that's God's problem and His job. It's His personal word, guarantee, and promise to you that He will place you there. You just need to show up on time, do your job, take of advantage of any additional training your employer offers, and live in a godly way that pleases Him by obeying His commands and quoting this scripture daily before you begin your work day. When the God of all the earth hears you quoting back to Him His own words, He is going to say to Himself, "That is my Word. I did say that, and I will honor my Word."

It's like a secret combination code, or a golden key that unlocks the heavens, and it is an ancient covenant language that He understands. If your job is to show a product, submit applications, or place phone calls to make sales, or whatever it is you're supposed to do, then do what you are required by your employer, and don't cut corners; the God of abundance will use every avenue available to bring you business and success. Don't even worry if you're behind during the quarter. Just trust Him; He will catch you up and completely surprise you and everyone around you.

All you need to do is daily ask the God of heaven to help you. For instance: "Heavenly Father and Lord Creator, I pray that you make me the head and not tail in my department this year, according to your promise in Deuteronomy 28:12–13, and please help me to continue to develop my godly character so I can be careful to obey your commands and be a blessing to others. Amen."

That's all you need say, but you need to be consistent and pray it daily, or at least once a week. If you miss a day in prayer, not to worry; just pick up where you left off.

Another prayer I like to say is this: "Heavenly Father, if I have been honorable in your sight, then please grant me confidence and unprecedented favor with all clients as I meet with them, because every customer can be challenging and unique. Additionally, your Word declares that You were with Moses and Aaron as they conducted the people's business, and the scriptures say that You personally taught them and instructed them what to say to Pharaoh and his officials. So, I pray now that You will be with me also as You were with them and teach my heart and mouth what to say as I meet with each new client, so I can be successful by helping others and enjoy your prosperity. Amen."

What the business world may not realize is that the God of heaven controls everything that happens on the earth. He causes the rain to fall, so the trees and plants can get the water they need to live and grow: "I will make them and the places all around My hill a blessing; and I will cause showers to come down in their season; there shall be showers of blessing. Then the trees of the field shall yield their fruit, and the earth shall yield her increase" (Ezekiel 34:26 NKJV). He controls all the seasons, including the sun as it rises and sets each day. He satisfies the desire of every living thing, and He is the one that causes the birds to migrate north and south each year. Psalm 145:16 (NIV) says, "You open your hand and satisfy the desires of every living thing."

The Lord is the one who gives food to the lions in Africa and all animals around the world. He controls and directs the wind and the weather; He controls everything, including the orbits of planets and heavenly bodies. Listen to me: If you pray this prayer daily and consistently, do your best to walk in integrity and Godliness, and work hard for your employer, He will direct the business traffic right to your doorstep. You will be left utterly stunned and amazed. Because it's not your job to become number one; it's His promise to you to make you number one, the lead person in your department, your office, your company. You will become the head and not the tail, as He promises in this scripture, and you will thank Him once you get there and actually see it happen. He will make good on His promise, for He is not a man who should lie: "God is not a man, that He should lie, nor a son of man, that He should repent. Has He said, and will He not do? Or has He spoken, and will He not make it good?" (Numbers 23:19 NKJV).

As I stated, all you need to do is show up on time for work, do everything you're asked by your employer, be ethical in the process, quote this magical scripture daily, which is a reminder to God, and then trust Him to bring it to pass. You are not going to believe your sales results when you invite the Almighty Creator's power and presence into your life every day to help you. The Lord is the one who really controls everything. He will provide all you need so you can meet your deadlines and make those impossible and ridiculous sales quotas your company expects from you.

How do I know this? Because I have been there, and He has done it for me countless times. It's supernatural, wonderful, and remarkable, and it's in the Bible; it has worked for me time after time, and it will work for you. I became the number one banker and manager for several years in different industries employing this technique; no one could figure out how I was able to do it. It comes right out of the Bible, my friend, and it was God doing it through me and for me, and He will do it for you also. Basically, you are using all the tools and training your employer is giving you, along with all the knowledge you have acquired in business school or elsewhere, and then you are partnering with God and the divine to help you succeed. You just need to stay humble when He pours out the rain on your land, and you see your sales soar like an eagle, and you become the head in your office. Do your part for your employer, put in an honest day's work, quote that magical scripture daily, show God you have done your homework by understanding His Word and promises, and live a godly lifestyle.

Now when you begin to receive this abundant blessing, make sure that you give, out of a generous heart, a certain portion to your favorite charity, and remember to financially support your local house of worship. This will help ensure that you never lack and that you have more than enough to be a blessing to others around you. You see, as you will find out, His ability, working through your availability, will bring about the miraculous. Now when this happens for you, and it will, make sure that you honor God by thanking him and by giving Him all the glory.

I would like to give you a short example to illustrate how God's power can work for you in the business world; this resource can not only help you keep your job, it will also help you stand out and shine. Even more importantly, God can assist you in becoming successful. The first thing you need to remember is that when you learn how to walk with Him, God's power and presence follows you wherever you go. This means whether you are at church, a movie theater, a park, your local supermarket, or the office, His presence is always with you. Joshua 1:9 (NKJV) says, "Have I not commanded you? Be strong and of good courage; do not be afraid, nor be dismayed, for the Lord your God is with you wherever you go."

I had worked for a reputable financial institution and, within in a couple of years, had risen to become the top banker at my branch. I accomplished this by working hard and using the techniques I previously mentioned. Naturally, over time, I was selected from among other great candidates to lead another branch as the head bank manager.

What the other managers and my colleagues did not know is that it was my daily practice to begin each day with prayer before I even left my home. Each morning in my prayer time, I asked the Lord to please grant me the wisdom I needed to solve the problems and challenges of the day and to help me lead the team with integrity and honor, while at the same time keeping a close eye on our sales goals and objectives. I also asked the Lord to bless the work of my hands and to help our branch to become the head and not the tail, in sales, service, and customer experience. Our primary objective was to help our customers with their financial needs, questions, and concerns while keeping the branch profitable and in compliance, because ultimately, we were there to serve our community.

It was a simple and fast but heartfelt prayer, and I would say it each morning before I left for work. On the day I was promoted, I was asked to take over a certain branch that had special challenges and areas of improvement that needed to be addressed over the next several months. It was rated ninth of the ten banks in my district. I really had my work cut-out for me, but I was not intimidated in the least. In fact, I was looking forward to the challenge ahead, especially because I was in a new position.

My faith in God gave me some comfort and peace; however, I was under intense pressure and on a fast learning curve, which included multiple meetings on a regular basis and a dozen conference calls each week. This meant I had to learn my new job while simultaneously solving the current problems, keeping the branch on track for meeting its goals, and preventing it from further decline. I got to work each morning before anyone and was typically the last one to leave. Each morning, I carefully reviewed the reports to see where we stood in terms of our sales goals and figured out which areas needed improvement. I spent much of my time asking myself what else I could do to bring in new customers and increase business; I sought creative ways to address the areas where our branch was not performing well.

In this prayer time at home, I regularly talked to the Lord about any work-related problems I was experiencing. I had to be patient and persistent, but within a few days or weeks, depending on the nature of problem, the answers came to me about how to resolve each issue. Some of those solutions came from other colleagues and managers I reached out to, but others required me to research and do some digging. And some of the answers honestly came right to my mind later that day after I prayed.

The executives I reported to were another great resource. They were always helpful and supplied me and my staff with their expertise and experience, which came from a wealth of knowledge acquired from being in the industry for many years. This assistance was just a phone call away, and it aided us tremendously. In less than eight months, this poorly performing and failing branch rose to the number one position in our district in all three areas: sales, service, and customer satisfaction. Can you believe that? I did not do it alone. On the contrary, I had a lot of help, but it was a divine partnership at work with God guiding me and meeting us halfway.

Our employees worked just as hard as I did, putting the new

expectations in place. And as the old saying goes, your company is only as good as your employees. We did our part, which meant showing up on time, putting in an honest day's work, fulfilling our job descriptions, taking advantage of additional training and workshops, and leading with integrity. But this story gets even better, because a year later, our branch (which had been ranked seventy-eighth out of one hundred banks in the Bay area) was now ranked number two companywide.

This achievement typically takes years to accomplish, but with God's power and divine help, it only took one year. Even I was surprised; I did not expect that to happen. Again, you need to know that this was not luck, magic, chance, or a coincidence. These institutions measure daily performance using various metrics and models, so this improvement demonstrates how the power of God, working in partnership with your commitment, can make wonders happen in the lives of those who obey, trust, and walk with Him. If you are a stockbroker or are employed selling financial services or are in the insurance business or any kind of a sales position, imagine what God can do for you when you live a life that is dedicated and surrendered to Him.

A Fisherman's Story

I would like to close this chapter by telling you a short story about a business-minded fisherman. You see, Peter and his companions, Thomas and Nathanael, knew from years of experience how to catch fish; it was their profession. In John 21, we see them fishing all night in order to catch enough so they could support themselves and their families, but they were unsuccessful and caught nothing that night. As morning approached, they saw someone on the shore, who turned out later to be Jesus.

The Lord then said to them, "Have you caught any fish?"

Feeling exhausted and disappointed, they answered, "No."

Jesus said to them, "Cast your nets on the right side of the boat, and you will find some fish."

They did as the Lord instructed them, and immediately God sent them a great multitude of fish. There were so many, in fact, that they couldn't bring the net into the boat; the fish were so heavy, the boat could have sunk. The Bible records that there were over 153 large fish that the Lord directed into that fishnet. I am more than certain that these individuals met their goals and quotas for the quarter. All that these business-minded people had to do was to trust God, and He provided everything they needed. You see, the way God directed all those large fish into the fisherman's net is the same way He will direct all the business, sales, and customers you need right to you. He has done it for me many times, and He will do it for you, as well. You just need to do your part, which is to call upon His name and learn to walk in His power by inviting Him into your life daily and then trust Him to bring it to pass. He will keep his promise.

For with God nothing will be impossible.

— Luke 1:37 (NKJV)

Giving up on Life and the God of Hope

May the God of Hope fill you with all joy and peace as you trust in him, so that you may overflow with hope by the power of the Holy Spirit.

—Romans 15:13 (NIV)

There are times in our lives when we feel down, discouraged, and depressed due to life's circumstances; we really believe in our heart that there is no hope, and we sense there is nowhere to turn, and the problem is just not resolvable. You may even feel paralyzed with fear and want to end your life; you may reach the conclusion that it's just not worth living anymore.

I felt this way in the past. I read reports in the news every year about how someone just gave up on life and committed suicide. This includes popular celebrities, rich executives, well-known public figures, students, and average people. How tragic and sad. When I see those reports on the news, I say to myself, if they only knew the God of hope (which just happens to be one of the Lord's many names). If they only understood that He is just waiting to help, they would never have gone down that dark path. I want to tell you that when you feel you are at the end of the road and are overwhelmed and stressed, regardless of what the problem is, you need to know that although the pain is real, the feeling of hopelessness is only an illusion. It's temporary.

My foster dad used to say to me when I was a kid, "This too shall pass," whenever he saw me discouraged and disheartened. And guess what? The hurt, pain, and loss always did pass. I eventually got over it, no matter what it was, and I came out stronger on the other end.

You may be going through a season of testing ordained by God, and you need to realize that you cannot have a testimony without a test. It's never easy to suffer losses and go through difficult problems, but they are there to help shape your character and destiny by making you stronger, well-rounded, and better prepared for what's coming next. You come out of those situations more refined and ready for the next challenge on your journey through life. If you didn't know it, I will let you in on a secret: God is in the character-building business, and He is always stretching us and challenging us to grow in different areas, which includes our physical, mental, and spiritual well-being. He will never give you anything you cannot handle without His help. Just call upon His name as you go through these fiery trials, and He will show up strong and help you get through it.

Everyone goes through losses, problems, hardships, and misfortunes in life. It's normal, so relax; it's not the end of the road or the end of the world. God may be preparing you for a new beginning, which will keep your life interesting and exciting. It's kind of like turning the page in a new chapter in your life story. The Lord is still in control and on His throne, and He will see you through it all. At times, what can be more important than the loss or the problem is how you respond to it. God is interested in your response and is observing you and watching carefully to see how you react to circumstances. Will you trust Him no matter what you are faced with? Will you become bitter, or will your actions show Him that you are ready for the next challenge, which will bring with it more rewards and greater responsibilities? Your reaction to the test may determine what the next challenge will be.

Keep in mind that with every new level you encounter, there will be a new devil you're going to have to deal with. When you have an exam at school, the teacher is usually silent while you're taking the test, but she or he is there at the end of the exam to see how you did. You may feel all alone, as if God is not there, as you go through your testing, but you need to know that like the silent teacher in the classroom, He is there the whole time. He actually helps you along the way. Whether you're aware of it or not, a book is being written about your life, so why not give Him a great resume and story to review?

No matter how bad the situations is, I always respond in faith by trusting God to work it out, and I try not to worry too much about what has happened. In prayer, I give the problem to Him and then visualize putting the issue into His hands. I do my part to resolve it, if possible, and then let go and let Him work it out. I often say to myself during these difficult and uncertain times that perhaps I've been called into a wilderness experience, as our Lord was and as the people of God were, and I am required to go through this testing, but He eventually will show me the way out. I figure there is a lesson

I am required to learn, so I always pray to help me learn it quickly, so I can get out of that situation and move on.

Oftentimes, God will not get rid of the problem for you or circumvent you around it, but He will deliver you through it, as He did for many others in the Bible. As I mentioned in the beginning of this book, I met the Creator personally. He is as real as you and I are, and you need to know that He is the God of hope. He does not want you ending your life or giving up prematurely on whatever test comes your way. You are here in part to experience new things and to grow as an individual and spiritual being. He is there to help you through every challenge and obstacle, and if you will just trust Him and hold on for a little while longer and earnestly pray to Him, He will prove Himself to you and help you out of whatever situation you find yourself stuck in.

We often create our own problems with the choices and decisions we make, and there are often severe consequences, but nevertheless, He understands and is forgiving. He knows that we are not perfect, and that we are going to make mistakes along the way, so He is there to help us out of it. God also wants you to be practical, so it doesn't hurt to seek help from organizations and people He has placed around you.

Perhaps you just lost your job or your wife/husband/girlfriend/boyfriend has just walked out on you. Maybe you're feeling all alone or have experienced a major setback or found yourself in jail or have lost a loved one or something very dear to you. I can tell you from personal experience that God can be trusted to help you. You just need to call upon His name and learn to walk with Him. You may need to exercise some restraint, patience, and faith in the interim period, but be patient. Don't end your life, give up on that dream, get even with someone, or commit suicide just because you're feeling hopeless. Give God a chance to work the problem out; give Him time to help you solve the problem.

Don't give up so easily; don't throw in the towel. Your life is worth living, and you have come too far; you still have a bright future ahead of you, no matter what the situation looks like or what you think you've lost. You may not always get the thing back that you lost, as I found out the hard way, but He will send you something even better that will make you much happier and will also heal you of the pain and the loss in the process.

The God of hope will not let you down, so give Him a season to turn the situation around for you. Over the years, He has delivered me from all kinds of negative circumstances you would find hard to believe, and He will do the same for you. No problem is too big or hard for Him to resolve. If you're feeling suicidal, don't give up; just call upon His name and give Him a chance to turn things around for you. You need to be aware that God moves within the seasons of your life when He knows you're ready. If you truly give Him an opportunity, He will keep his promise and make up to you every setback, loss, and disappointment you've ever experienced, and in the end, He will give you double for all the trouble you went through. You can take that to the bank, and that statement is coming from a former successful banker. In fact, in the end, you won't even remember the bad times or the losses but will only reflect on the good times, the wins, and the numerous blessings.

Sinner's Prayer

Dear God, I am a sinner. I'm sorry for my sin; please forgive me and help me. I believe Jesus Christ is Your Son and that He died for my sins and You raised Him to life. I want to invite Him into my heart and lead my life.

In Jesus' name, I pray. Amen.

Names of God: Meaning and Scripture Reference

English Names Hebrew Names

The King of Kings
Revelation 19:11–16, 1 Timothy 6:15
Elohim (God, one of strength or power)
Genesis 1:1, Psalm 19:1

The Lord of Lords
Psalm 136:3, 1 Timothy 6:15
Adonai (Lord, Master)
Malachi 1:6

The Ancient of Days
(The God of ancient times)
Daniel 7:9–10
El Shaddai (Lord God Almighty)
Genesis 17:1, Psalm 91:1

The Most High God
Genesis 14:18, Psalm 78:35
Jehovah-Yahweh (reference to God's divine salvation)
Genesis 2:4

The Lord of Hosts
(God as Lord over earthly or heavenly armies)
Isaiah 54:5, Jeremiah 15:16
Jehovah Nissi (The Lord my banner)
Exodus 17:15

The King of Glory
Psalm 24:8, 10
Jehovah Rapha (The Lord that heals)
Exodus 15:26

The Lord God Almighty
Genesis 17:1, Revelation 1:8
Jehovah Sabbaoth (The Lord of hosts)
Isaiah 6:1–3

The Everlasting God
Isaiah 40:28
Jehovah Shammah (The Lord is present)
Ezekiel 48:35

The Lord, The Lord God
Isaiah 40:28
El Elyon (The Most High God)
Deuteronomy 8:7, Genesis 14:17–20

The Fountain of Living Waters
(The fountain of life)
Jeremiah 17:13
Jehovah Jireh (The Lord will provide)
Genesis 22:13–14

I Am, I Am That I Am
Exodus 3:14
Jehovah Tsidkenu (The Lord our righteousness)
Jeremiah 23:6

The Alpha and Omega
(The beginning and the end)
Revelation 1:8, 22:13
El Olam (The everlasting God)
Isaiah 40:28–31

Abba Father, Heavenly Father
Similar to Daddy
Mark 14:36, Luke 11:13, Matthew 6:26
Jehovah Shalom (The Lord of peace)
Judges 6:24

The God of the whole earth
Isaiah 54:5, Psalm 47:7
Jehovah Maccaddeshem (The Lord who sanctifies you)
Exodus 31:13

The King of Angels
(Not in scripture but implied)
Jehovah Rohi (The Lord is my shepherd)
Psalm 23:1

God, God the Father
Ephesians 4:6, 1 Peter 1:3
El Roi (The strong one who sees)
Genesis 16:13

The Creator, The Almighty
Isaiah 40:28, 42:5; Revelations 1:8

The God of Hope
Romans 5:13

The God of Abraham, Isaac, and Jacob
Matthew 22:32

About the Author

Luis A. Gonzalez has been active in various Christian ministries over the past twenty-five years, which include outreach to the homeless community, ushering ministry, church council, Thanksgiving and holiday relief efforts, back-to-school programs for kids, and Bible studies. He has a bachelor's degree in management and an MBA from Golden Gate University and is also a licensed airplane mechanic/technician. He was a corporate securities paralegal and worked closely with numerous attorneys forming corporations and preparing IPOs, mergers, and acquisitions. He also was a bank manager, selling financial services and products. He is an entrepreneur and currently the president and CEO of Rose's Cleaning Corporation, based in Silicon Valley.

Contact Information:
Address:
P. O. Box 993
Palo Alto, CA 94302

Email:
walkinginthepower@gmail.com

Website:
walkinginthepower.org

CPSIA information can be obtained
at www.ICGtesting.com
Printed in the USA
BVHW070816200519
548790BV00010B/247/P